"*Walk Toward Wealth* is a must-read for people who want to learn how to create their luck with an income-producing methodology."

- JEFF SAUT, Managing Partner, Saut Strategy

"Kevin simplifies complex investment concepts with such confidence and ease ... I didn't want this book to end."

- JACKIE DeANGELIS, FOX Business Network correspondent

"Kevin's covered call, risk-managed approach to growing wealth is a great strategy for taking the emotion out of investing."

- GARY KAMINSKY, Former Capital Markets Editor, CNBC, and Former Vice Chairman, Morgan Stanley

WALK TOWARD WEALTH

WALK
TOWARD
WEALTH

The Two Investing Strategies
Everyone Should Know.

KEVIN SIMPSON

MERACK PUBLISHING

Published and distributed by:
Merack Publishing, San Diego, CA.
Printed in Canada through Bookmark
FIRST EDITION

Designed by Ryan Dawson.
Photography by Chris Urso.

Library of Congress Control Number: 2021924311
Simpson, Kevin
Walk Toward Wealth

Hardcover 978-1-957048-07-9

This book is dedicated to my wife, JoAnna,

my son, Jack,

and my dog, Dallas.

Thank you for always encouraging me to reach higher

and to strive for perfection.

CONTENTS

///////////////////////

K evin and I both come from hard-working families who, just a few generations ago, humbly made their way from Europe to the United States to passionately pursue the American Dream.

While they proudly ended up as auto mechanics, schoolteachers, crane operators, and stay-at-home moms — not rich by any means — our families have heart, worked hard, and budgeted, which helped us establish a value system and sense of self-worth that can't be measured in dollar signs.

Our blue-collar and middle-class upbringings may not have paved our way with silver spoons, but they showed us that drive and determination can take you places.

You don't get to pick your family of origin, or where or when you're born. A lot of things in life are serendipitous. When it comes to creating wealth and building financial independence, you don't have to rely on either. In this book, Kevin lays out in clear language and simple steps how you can build wealth based on the knowledge of seasoned portfolio managers honed over decades.

Until now, the benefits of portfolio hedging haven't been accessible to the public at large. Instead, this knowledge has been held close by professional wealth managers and wealthy financiers. The democratization of wealth, full transparency, long-term thinking, and a consistent strategy are all aspects of money management that we also believe in at SkyBridge.

It doesn't matter if you're familiar with options strategies or don't yet understand the foundation of buying and selling stocks. All you need is curiosity, a desire to learn, and discipline to apply the strategies taught here.

The two important strategies Kevin details — writing covered calls and purchasing proven, dividend-paying equities — can help improve your investment returns through steady gains by focusing on investing for the long term and walking toward wealth instead of trying to get rich quick. His focus on dividend-paying, blue-chip equities is especially timely and prudent in our current low interest rate environment.

Kevin has the "X factor" for being successful: He's not afraid to make decisions. Why? Because he stays true to his investing philosophy that you'll learn about in the pages to come. I don't believe in money managers who are bottlenecks ... where every decision comes from one person. Having a disciplined, rules-based process allows Kevin to show you through real-life examples the methodology behind the decision-making.

In investing and life, we have knowns, unknowns, and unknown unknowns. When I left my first job out of Harvard Law School at Goldman Sachs to run a money management firm, I was a naïve 32-year-old living in the mid-1990s who confused brains with the bull market. My foray into politics as a leverage mechanism to network and grow my career in finance, evolved into letting my ego and pride take me somewhere not well-suited for my personality. I've learned there are things you think you know with great confidence that you get wrong.

Kevin works to remove emotion from investing with his tried-and-true, disciplined process to help limit ego-driven mistakes and manage risk. Every decision to invest or not is based on his rules-based approach that remains the same no matter what's happening in the market. As you'll learn, knowing what to do, instead of focusing on the cause of high volatility or a market correction, is key.

When it comes to decision-making, conviction is good. Overconfidence and ego are not. Don't ever put your pride and ego into your decision making. Whether you're a seasoned investor or just getting started, this part of the human condition is the great equalizer.

More important than money, it's the human condition that connects us all. With wealth, we can do things for ourselves, families, communities, and the world. Beyond wealth, recognize that you're on a journey and enjoy it.

- Anthony Scaramucci
Founder and Managing Partner of SkyBridge Capital

"Invest and save wisely."

– Cecilia Kopcinski

C ecilia didn't invent value-investing, and she wasn't the Oracle of Omaha, yet her words resonate with the same telling veracity of Benjamin Graham's or Warren Buffet's. Who was she? Cecilia was my grandmother. And although she (Babcia, as we lovingly called her), along with my grandfather, Pop-Pop, fell squarely in the lower-middle class demographic, their fiscal responsibility and shrewd approach to saving made them the richest people I knew.

Surprisingly, I received a letter from Babcia just a couple years ago that was written 30 years prior. At the time, she purchased a zero-coupon bond in my name with a 2020 maturity date. When it matured, I received a $10,000 check and a handwritten letter:

Dear Kevin,

You know we love you very much, and hope you spend this money wisely. I hope you appreciate this act of love as we both worked hard to earn it. You know your grandfather was only a laborer at the Frankfort arsenal. I handled the money and invested and saved wisely, because it always gave us so much joy to give to our children. We love you all. God bless you, dear Kevin.

- Babcia + Pop-Pop

This is an incredibly powerful life lesson — one that bears repeating

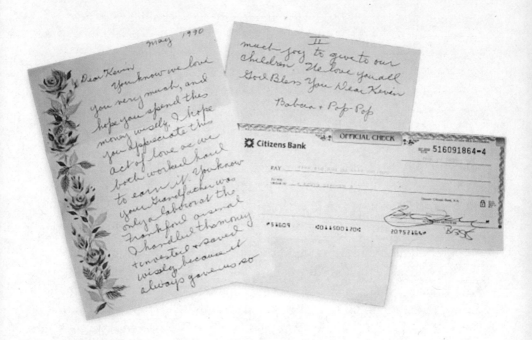

to yourself, your clients, and even to your family, no matter the market environment or pressing issues at hand. It's always relevant to share the importance of having a long-term timeframe, committing to an investment strategy, and allowing the power of compounding to do its work.

Where it all began

During the stock market crash in 1987, I was a senior in high school, and we had very little business education as part of the curriculum. The crash dominated the news cycle for weeks. I asked my father, a schoolteacher, about it, but it wasn't his area of expertise. My mom had her hands full with me and my younger brother, Keith, and didn't participate in the stock market either. But I was immediately interested and relentless in my pursuit of knowledge about the markets, going back to the crash of 1929.

When I was in high school, we didn't have the internet, so this research was all done in a library. It was incredibly fascinating. The more I learned, the more I wondered, "Why didn't anyone see the crash coming? Why was the market correction in 1987 a surprise?" And that's how I became passionate about the markets.

Where we are

My goal in writing this book is to provide everyone, from the ordinary investor to the experienced wealth advisor, insight from the most seasoned portfolio managers. For a long time, the benefits of portfolio hedging have only been accessible to professional wealth managers and wealthy financiers. In this book, I'll share two important strategies to improve your investment returns: writing covered calls and purchasing proven, dividend-paying equities.

The first of these strategies, writing covered calls, is designed to provide additional income, and they reduce volatility along the way.

The other strategy, purchasing proven, dividend-paying equities, is one of the secrets to obtaining regular income. I use easy-to-understand language to show you how you can create real wealth for yourself. This book is for anyone who's eager to learn ways to grow their wealth. It doesn't matter where you fit on the investing knowledge spectrum. And as the title suggests, my focus is on investing for the long term — making steady gains — instead of foolishly chasing the market.

All you need is an open mind and a willingness to learn. With those two qualities in place, your next steps involve the disciplined application of the strategies discussed. Creating wealth and building financial independence are not limited by inheritance or luck. We live in a time when you can build wealth through the consistent application of time tested, proven investment strategies.

You may be wondering how this book differs from others you may have seen, or how the advice it offers is different from what you frequently hear from financial pundits. To be clear, this is a strategic plan that adds value to your long-term investments and isn't a get-rich-quick scheme.

Maybe you're intrigued by covered calls. Or perhaps regular dividend income appeals to you. Whatever the reason, I'm grateful for your interest in creating a better return on your invested wealth. The steps you'll learn here work in both bull and bear markets.

As Babcia taught me, investing and saving wisely is a legacy for our loved ones. I hope you take away an abundance of knowledge from what I'm about to share with you and pass these ideas to future generations or people you care about. After all, investing wisely and sharing our success with others is a matter of love and pays the ultimate dividend — joy!

Thank you, Babcia and Pop-Pop.

"The best way to measure
your investing success
is not by whether you're
beating the market, but
by whether you've put in
place a financial plan and
a behavioral discipline that
are likely to get you where
you want to go."

- Benjamin Graham, economist, professor, investor,
and author of "The Intelligent Investor"

It may come as a surprise that information on wealth-building isn't available to everyone. Lack of investment knowledge is actually quite common among people of all ages, in almost every profession. It's not anything to be ashamed of, but it's something that can hold you back from reaping the best returns on your hard-earned savings. This is where I'm eager to congratulate you for picking up this book. Your desire to learn is a testament to not only your personal inquisitiveness, but an excellent reason to be optimistic about your future.

I've been investing professionally since 1992, when I joined W.H. Newbold's Son & Co., shortly after graduating from The George Washington University with a degree in finance. Subsequently, I worked for seven years at Wheat First Butcher Singer (later, Wells Fargo) where I helped institutions and high-net-worth individuals plan and achieve their financial goals, utilizing stock, bond, and option-based strategies. After this, I worked at Sterling Financial before opening my own wealth-management firm, Capital Wealth Planning, in Naples, Florida, in 2005. It was here that I began to practice the strategies outlined in this book and apply institutional investment management strategies to diversified equity and option portfolios.

While politics and opinion are woven into everyday financial news, we're going to disregard those concerns. Instead, we're going to focus on how to make the most of your investments, the same way a professional money manager would — through the conservative income-oriented combination of covered calls and dividends.

We will avoid speculative talk about the latest and greatest "hot" stock and casino-like investing in the stock market. News cycles tend to be more about moving in and out of stocks than investing in great companies. It's unfortunate because the latter is key to being successful. I'm passionate about teaching others to invest in individual stocks. It's an imperfect-yet-consistent way to receive profit streams from public companies in return for the capital invested in them. While stock prices and portfolio values fluctuate in the short term, quality investments tend to steadily appreciate in the long term.

Famous value investor Benjamin Graham made an important distinction between investing and speculating in his book, *The Intelligent Investor.* He said, "An investment operation is one which, upon thorough analysis, promises safety of principal and an adequate return. Operations not meeting these requirements are speculative."

Graham also observed how intelligent, serious individuals who had carefully accumulated wealth through hard work and diligence were often indifferent and lackadaisical when it came to investing those same hard-earned dollars. Graham pointed this out saying, "It is amazing to see how many capable businessmen try to operate in Wall Street with complete disregard to the sound principles through which they have gained success in their own undertakings."

To his point, far too many individuals haphazardly buy and sell financial instruments they know little about, frittering away wealth that took years — and often the majority of their lives — to build.

Investors who speculate are often undisciplined, erratic, and impatient, wanting immediate returns without understanding how the stock market works. These investors fail to realize that time and quality investments are your best friends when it comes to increasing your net worth.

I'm not interested in wild speculations or rash decision-making based on impulsive choices, website chatter, or adrenaline rushes. Instead of trying to interpret the varying and often conflicting information that can push people toward buying or selling any in-favor or out-of-favor stocks, we're going to focus on the two time-tested and proven investment strategies.

It's worth repeating that investing in a diversified portfolio of great companies at reasonable prices, holding them (or occasionally replacing one), receiving dividend payments, and collecting covered call income, steadily builds wealth.

I'm excited you're here. Let's get started.

"The pessimist complains about the wind, the optimist expects it to change, the realist adjusts the sails."

- William Arthur Ward, motivational writer

I n its original state, the stock market was designed to create wealth and help entrepreneurs build businesses out of their enterprising ideas. This, in turn, would benefit the economy. There's no doubt that the stock market is a remarkable, thriving engine that drives economies all over the world. If you wish to grow your money, in my opinion, investing is the best way to achieve genuine returns that beat inflation.

Yet in the last decade, the stock market has faced skepticism and derision thanks to the struggles that arose from the 2008 recession — a recession that had detrimental impact on individual retirement accounts and devalued 401(k) funds by nearly 50% for millions of Americans. This instilled fear and wariness of the investment market and caused individual investors to yank funds out of their 401(k) plans and IRAs, exacerbating the financial meltdown.

Despite the subsequent economic contraction that the 2008 great recession (and COVID in 2020) triggered, we should remember that, by its nature, the stock market will rise and fall over time. The key principle: Don't let fear of fluctuating stock prices drive you to withdraw your cash when stock prices plummet.

In instances where stock prices fall, fixed-income investments (i.e., certificates of deposit [CD] and savings) may seem like good options for people who feel the market is too risky. It may also feel like the right time to liquidate holdings. However, keeping your money "under your mattress," as the saying goes, doesn't benefit you in the long run. Your cash declines in value compared to inflation, and your returns miss out on the dividends you would have received had you held onto your stock investments. In addition, historic yields on fixed investments render lower returns than stock investments.

If you go back to August 2018, CD or money market funds offered very small returns. A five-year CD yield topped out at 2.0%. As we just learned, that's barely enough to cover the rate of inflation, historically speaking.

Another way to look at this is to visualize the value of your dollar in the future. If you put $5,000 into a CD, at the end of the five-year term, you'd be lucky if that money was worth $5,000 in real value once adjusted for inflation.

On the other hand, if you were to take the same principal of $5,000 and invest it in a portfolio of individual stocks, exchange-traded funds (ETFs), and/or mutual funds, you have the potential to see a much better return on investment, where you'd overcome inflation and genuinely create wealth. Your investment portfolio benefits from compounding over time at a higher rate of return. This is probably a good time to concede that there are no guarantees with the stock market. Stocks don't always go straight up. Sometimes they go down.

> **Good to know**
>
> Most CD and savings accounts offer very low interest rates that, at best, barely keep up with inflation.

This would apply even if you invest a larger amount upfront in your CD or online savings account (in our example, maximizing at 1.8-2.0%) for a shorter period of time. Interest rates for CDs have been going down year after year. If you locked away your cash in a CD, when you pulled it out, the principal and interest earned could still be worth less than the original purchasing power of your principal due to inflation.

In Figure 1, you can see how the rate of return for CDs have been steadily decreasing over the years. You can also see how it doesn't even meet the

Income earned by $100,000 investment
6 month CD

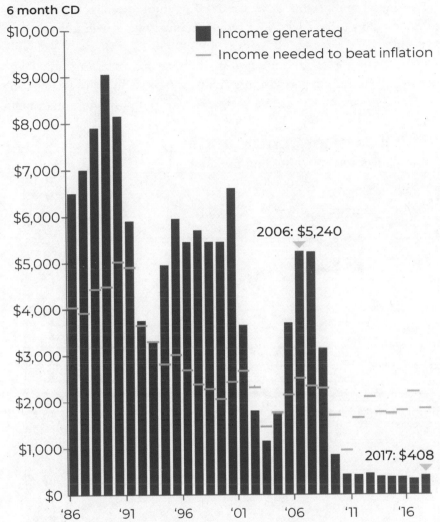

Fig 1. Sources: FactSet. J.P. Morgan Asset Management, Bankrate.com. Data is current as of July 31, 2018.

rate of inflation in recent years. A $100,000 investment in a CD in 2017 would have paid only $408 interest in six months.

If you kept your money in a diversified investment account over the same time period, you could have experienced a return of 7% on the lower end.

That would translate to $3,500 in profit for the same six months — considerably more than your $408 in a CD. This amount can increase through compounding as you keep your money in investments over a longer time period.

Markets, however, are subject to volatility, so your investment could go down in a six-month period and then up the next six months. By investing for a longer period, you can make up losses in your portfolio, and through

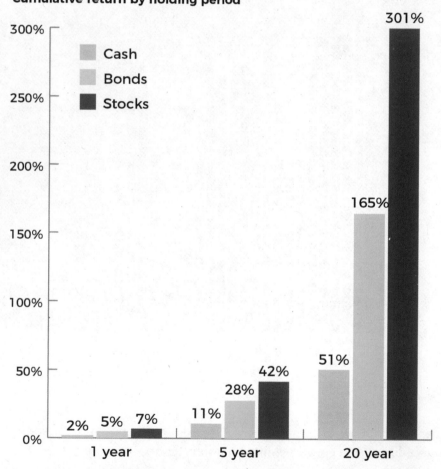

The power of compounding
Cumulative return by holding period

Fig 2. Sources: FactSet, BLS, Standard & Poor's, and J.P. Morgan Asset Management. Data as of July 31, 2018.

dollar-cost averaging (systematically investing equal amounts, spaced out over regular intervals, regardless of price), earn a higher rate of return over time.

If you stand steady when the market dips and keep your money in your investment portfolio, you can achieve significant gains in the long run. In fact, some of the wealthiest individuals in the world, including Warren Buffett, have amassed their fortunes through the virtue of patience. Buffett has consistently bought shares in several high-quality, well-managed businesses at a fair price that he opted to hold on to indefinitely.

While many so-called "experts" have debated this approach, the results speak for themselves. For Buffett and/or any investor who truly wishes to grow their wealth, owning stocks is more than staring at analytics, charts, or financial data releases. Instead, it's about ownership — having a real interest and pride in owning a piece of a business that will deliver your share of present and future profits (and sometimes losses). It represents a steadfast, long-term commitment to ride out volatility and trust that management will conquer the headwinds that come up from time to time.

CD compounding
10-year return

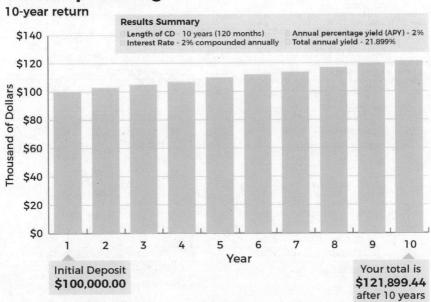

Fig 3. Source: Bankrate. Data as of August 27, 2018.

BACKSTORY:

The names change, the stocks change, the companies change, but the methodology of finding great investments never does.

It was through trial and error that I uncovered the investing strategies I'm sharing with you. In the early days of my career, and during the creation of Capital Wealth Planning, I made every mistake possible. When you think of an overnight success taking 30 years ... that's really the case with our portfolios, as well.

There wasn't anything special with how I thought about the markets back then — or today. I keep things really simple. And to

this day, I stick to a rules-based approach.

Simple doesn't mean bad or even stupid, it just means keeping your head down and staying true to your principles. It entails investing in companies that have great balance sheets, solid fundamentals, good management, great products, supply chains, the ability to increase their prices during inflationary periods, and the agility to navigate recessionary periods because they manage well and have free cash flow on hand.

I look at owning stock in companies that tend to increase earnings over time, and we also look at companies that increase their dividends because they can afford that increase through earnings growth. In general, you'll see their stock prices appreciate, as well. That's the true success and measure of investing — consistently producing solid returns, not trying to hit a home run.

This method has made many, many professional investors extremely wealthy over time. It's not a question of trying to reinvent the wheel.

Portfolio returns
Equities vs. equity and fixed income blend

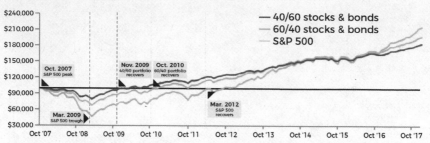

20-year Annualized Returns by Asset Class (1999-2019)
Investor commitment is key – returns are lost by missing out on even the 10 best performing days in a 20-year time span.

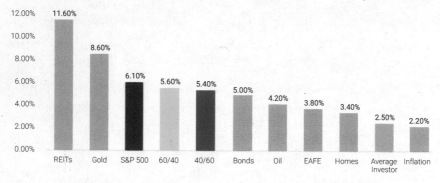

Fig 4. Source: J.P. Morgan Asset Management; (Top) Barclays, Bloomberg, FactSet, Standard & Poor's; (Bottom) Dalbar Inc. Indices used are as follows: REITS: NAREIT Equity REIT Index, EAFE: MSCI EAFE, Oil: WTI Index, Bonds: Bloomberg Barclays U.S. Aggregate Index, Homes: median sale price of existing single-family homes, Gold: USD/troy oz., Inflation: CPI, 60/40: A balanced portfolio with 60% invested in S&P 500 Index and 40% invested in high-quality U.S. fixed income, represented by the Bloomberg Barclays U.S. Aggregate Index. The portfolio is rebalanced annually. Average asset allocation investor return is based on an analysis by Dalbar Inc., which utilizes the net of aggregate mutual fund sales, redemptions and exchanges each month as a measure of investor behavior. Returns are annualized (and total return where applicable) and represent the 20-year period ending 12/31/17 to match Dalbar's most recent analysis.

Potential portfolio growth

Here's a hypothetical example of a diversified portfolio over a 10-year period, with a starting investment of $100,000. In all three portfolio allocations, the rate of return is significantly higher, bringing in additional earnings of roughly

$60,000 to $90,000 on the initial investment. Wouldn't you have preferred to make more cash on your investment?

	5%	10%
10 years	$162,889	$259,374
20 years	$265,330	$672,750
30 years	$432,194	$1,744,940

Investing for the same period of time — 10 years — could give you a profit of more than $60,000 at a 5% rate of return, or more than $150,000 at a 10% rate of return. As you can see, the difference is staggering — especially after 20 or 30 years. In this hypothetical example, even if you choose not to contribute another penny to your account, you would have more than $1.7 million in your retirement savings after 30 years simply by earning a higher rate of return. And as you can see, the faster your money grows, the more you'll have when you retire, or better yet, the earlier you can plan to retire. When it comes to the power of compounding, time is certainly on our side.

Risk happens

Do we stay safe and forgo earnings, or do we endure some risk for the opportunity to earn more money?

The choice is clear

Investing is clearly the winner in terms of growing your wealth. When you invest, you own a piece of a company or companies with the expectation that you'll get a return that's greater than what you put in. In terms of stocks, you're providing capital to a company, or you purchased shares on the open market, in return for a small ownership stake in the company.

Why isn't everyone doing this? Because investments come with risk, which can be scary. It's where rethinking your reaction to risk becomes critical.

As we can see in the examples in this chapter, if you place your money only in safe investments such as CDs, you won't see an appreciable return. You may be assured that your principal is intact, but it hasn't grown enough to keep up with inflation for future value, and hence your purchasing power when your CD comes of age could be less than what you started with.

Again, the dilemma worth rethinking is this: Do you keep your money in safe investments where there's no appreciable return, or do you invest in vehicles with greater return that bear risks during short- or long-term drops in the market? Do we stay safe and forgo earnings, or do we endure risk for the opportunity to earn more money? For the average investor, it's normal to feel stuck between a low-return rock and a high-risk hard place.

So, how do you grow your wealth?

Are these the only choices available for the average investor?

Fortunately, they aren't. You can enjoy the potential for substantial rates of return while keeping risk to a minimum writing covered calls on high-quality, blue-chip stocks. You can also generate consistent income off stocks you own and keep, through dividends.

In the next chapter, we'll take a deeper dive into the two key investing strategies that everyone should know.

Take notes and stay excited, because you're going to come out a savvy investor.

Key takeaway

Don't get stuck between a low-return rock and a high-risk hard place. You have choices to grow your wealth.

"Focus on value because most investors focus on outlook and trends."

- Sir John Templeton, American-British investor

While Wall Street investments bear risk, they are also the primary vehicle for growing your nest egg. News cycles are full of varying political opinion, market commentary, and polls, but the market itself is primarily driven by fundamentals.

By writing covered calls on dividend-paying stocks, you can earn:

- Dividends from stocks owned.
- Capital appreciation if the stocks rise in value.
- A premium, which is cash received from investors who buy the options you write or sell.

How dividend-paying stocks and covered calls work together

While writing covered calls may not be your parents' investment technique, it's a smart strategy and is used by experienced portfolio managers, successful high-net-worth individuals, and corporations.

Covered calls are the most fiscally conservative of option trades. While other forms of options trading carry significant risk, covered calls do not. In fact, they're designed to help offset stock risk by providing a modest gain from the call premiums. The key, of course, is to know what you're doing. That's what I'll teach you.

BACKSTORY:

It's not a question of inspiration for me, it's a fascination with the markets that started in 1987 and continues every day I wake up.

The stock market never has monotony. Every single day, every single minute, the news cycles are changing. The markets are affected by everything, whether it's geopolitical, local, or weather-related. So many things can affect the markets, which means it never gets boring. I wake up wondering what's going to happen today — and it's not always great. Sometimes it's really lousy. But it's never boring, and it's never the same.

Incorporating dividend-paying stocks

It's baffling how the average investor is willing to buy bonds and lend money to the U.S. treasury for less than 2% for a decade or more. This is such a low return on investment, and could even be flat or negative when you factor in the cost of inflation.

A better decision would be to place that cash in a diversified portfolio of dividend-paying stocks — our second strategy for growing wealth.

This advice might sound very basic, but most average investors aren't doing it. Simply put, make sure you're holding investments that pay dividends.

S&P 500

The Standard & Poor's 500 represents approximately 80% of the investible U.S. equity market. It measures changes in stock market conditions based on the average performance of 500 widely-held common stocks.

As Benjamin Graham wrote in *The Intelligent Investor* — a book Warren Buffett has described as the most influential and important book on investing — "Invest only if you would be comfortable owning a stock even if you had no way of knowing its daily share price."

Over the last 50 years, the highest 20% yielding stocks in the S&P 500 returned 14.2% per year. That means you could have doubled your money every five years. If you had been selective and invested in the 10 highest-yielding stock companies of the S&P 500, then your actual annual total return would have been 15.7%.

According to Fidelity Investments, 44% of the U.S. stock market return came from dividends from 1930 - 2010. Some periods generated larger returns, such as the 1970s, when dividends reaped 71% of returns.

Cashing in dividends offers terrific opportunities for growing your wealth, but they're not the only method for generating returns. Reinvesting your dividends and allowing the power of compounded interest to kick in can do wonders for the growth of your portfolio.

Nobel Prize-winning physicist Albert Einstein appreciated the power of compound interest. He said that money compounding "is the most powerful force in the universe." One of the best ways to compound your money is through investing in great companies that pay steadily and increase dividends.

Key takeaway

The two investing strategies we've outlined in this chapter — writing covered calls on a diversified portfolio and including dividend-paying stocks in your portfolio — are both smart strategies within your reach.

"The question isn't at what age I want to retire, it's at what income."

- George Foreman, boxing legend

In 1979, Nobel Prize winner Daniel Kahneman led a series of behavioral finance studies, known collectively as the Prospect Theory. He demonstrated how the human brain is instinctively wired to seek certainty over uncertainty, especially when dealing with money and loss-aversion.

The studies revealed that a majority of individuals had an overwhelming bias to choose a guaranteed $500 payout over receiving either $1,000 or nothing, based on the flip of a coin. As high as 84% of respondents chose the guaranteed return, despite an equivalent expected return. The study showed that people preferred certain gains over the prospect of having larger gains with more risk. This preference for certainty is even more interesting when you look at actual returns and investments over time.

Risk-averse investors naturally prefer more consistent returns over time. Yet, these investors have also discovered — to their surprise — that more consistent returns can compound to higher returns over time. If you, like a majority of investors, are risk-averse, you may want to consider adding a covered call strategy to your equity investment portfolio.

Covered call writing offers equity investors the opportunity to receive more stable returns and lower volatility than strictly-equity portfolios. In addition, the premium generated through the sale of the call options can provide a consistent income. A portfolio with a covered call strategy can provide an excellent way of reducing risk, adding supplemental income, and providing a form of modest downside protection.

What is a covered call?

In short, a covered call strategy is a fiscally conservative option strategy that offers an excellent method of generating additional income from your investment portfolio and modestly offsetting a stock's downside.

Covered call strategies can be a relatively conservative method of investing, where call options are used to reduce risk in the portfolio. This type of investing combines a traditional asset class (equities) with an alternative asset class (call options). The covered call strategy consists of collecting an upfront premium in cash by selling (or writing) a call option against an underlying stock at a predetermined strike price (fixed price at which the option owner can purchase the stock) and contract expiration (date at which the option becomes worthless if not exercised). The seller of the call option collects a premium for consideration in providing the buyer the right to purchase the underlying stock at the specified strike price. With a covered call strategy in place, you can modestly hedge in the case of a market downturn for your stock.

> **Bridging the gap**
>
> An effective covered call strategy on exchange-traded funds and dividend stocks can help bridge the ever-increasing savings gap retirees are facing.

This strategy is designed to generate income through the sale of call options and potential ownership of an equivalent number of underlying shares of stock. In exchange for the income generated by the sale of the call option, an investor agrees to sell the stock at a specific price for a fixed time period.

Covered calls can be used with stock that an investor owns in a margin, cash, IRA, or Keogh account (a tax-deferred pension plan for self-employed people or unincorporated businesses). Investors looking to take advantage of the benefits of covered-call investing have a range of opportunities, as basic as writing listed call options against individual equity

Retirement savings gap

Anticipated amount needed vs. actual savings, thousands

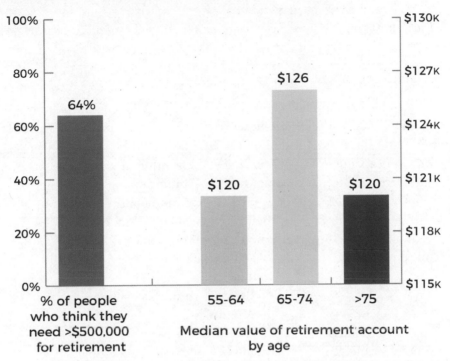

Source: J.P. Morgan Asset Management; 2017 Retirement Confidence Survey, Employee Benefit Research Institute and Greenwald & Associates; U.S. Data are as of July 31, 2018.

holdings, to purchasing more sophisticated covered call solutions through exchange-traded funds, mutual funds, and separately managed accounts.

Today more than ever, retirees and people approaching retirement are facing a savings gap due to low interest rates. Having additional forms of income is increasingly necessary. An effective covered call strategy on dividend stocks can help bridge that gap.

Having a covered call strategy is akin to a lease option to buy when renting out your property and getting a passive income stream separate from the equity value of the asset. In terms of stocks, this means that you can generate cash flow on your stock portfolio similar to a lease option in real estate, separate from your dividends, by selling covered calls.

This ability to earn money on your stock holdings can offer you income if your stock price goes down, which provides some loss protection for those shares. It's a conservative strategy that works well by letting you sell the right to purchase your stock at a price that's higher than its current price at some point down the road.

A covered call is an option strategy, and a call is an option. Let's start by explaining what options are and then dig into each of these terms.

Exploring options

An option is a contract by which you can buy or sell a specific underlying asset at a specified price within a predetermined time period. This asset could be a stock, an index, or an ETF. Options are also called derivatives because the value of an option is derived from the underlying asset. An option creates a legally binding contract. Trading options offers you additional ways to approach the market beyond just buying the stock outright (bullish) or shorting the stock (bearish). When you trade options, you can:

> ### Call option
>
> A contract which gives the owner the right to buy shares of stock at a stated price (strike price).

• Generate income on existing stocks in your portfolio.

• Purchase a stock at a discount to the market price.

• Purchase the right to buy a stock at a certain price without committing to full ownership costs.

• Protect individual stocks in your portfolio from large declines, or make more speculative directional bets on the market itself.

Covered calls are a form of option strategy with a primary investment goal of generating income, followed by providing some downside protection.

There are two sides to an option contract. On one end there is a buyer, and on the other end there is a seller. The buyer obtains certain rights, while the seller assumes certain obligations.

The buyer of an option purchases the right — but not the obligation — to either buy or sell the underlying stock at a specified price within the time frame of the option contract. If the option buyer chooses to take action on their right to buy or sell, this is known as exercising the option.

The seller of an option collects the cash paid by the buyer and is obligated to buy or sell the underlying stock at a specified price if the option is exercised. If the option buyer exercises the option, then the seller receives an assignment to fulfill the terms of the option.

Owning an option is different from a stock where you own shares in a company.

Options give you the potential to buy or sell — they essentially give you more choices. Having an option gives you the right, but not the obligation, to perform a certain action. If you own an option, you can also buy or sell the asset if you choose. You're not obligated to buy or sell, but enjoy the right to do so when you wish. You can also do nothing until the option expires. When the option expires, its value is gone, and your option contract is void. You establish a position in the underlying stock (known as a long or a short) only when you have exercised the option. Each option contract represents 100 shares of the underlying stock.

Two options: Calls and puts

A call option gives the contract owner/holder (the buyer of the call option) the right to buy the underlying stock at a specified price by the expiration date.

In investment terms, people who buy calls hope the stock price will increase before the option period expires.

A put option gives the contract owner the right to sell the underlying

Consider this example

Let's say that shares of Apple (AAPL) are trading at $150 per share. You feel the share price will rise over the next month or so.

Instead of buying actual shares of Apple stock, you could purchase an option (one option contract controls 100 shares of stock), to buy 100 shares at $160 per share at any time during the next 60 days.

That option might cost you $0.50 per share, or $50 total. If the price of Apple stock doesn't go above $160, you won't exercise the option. You don't want to pay more than you'd pay on the open market. In that case, you'll let the option expire for a loss.

On the other hand, if the price of Apple stock goes up to $165 per share, you could exercise your option, buy the owner's shares at $160 each, and enjoy a $4.50 per-share profit after the cost of the call (yes, that's hypothetical 9x return of your $50 investment).

stock at a specified price by the expiration date.

You might buy a call when you expect that the price of the underlying stock will go up. On the other hand, you might buy a put when you expect that the price of the underlying stock will go down.

Puts may sound counter-intuitive, so think of them this way: Puts are simply the option version of selling a stock short — if you think the price of a stock will fall, you could sell shares you don't currently own. If the price falls, you can buy those shares at a lower price, replace the shares you sold for a higher price, and pocket the difference as profit — or, if the trade goes your way directionally, you could simply sell the put for a profit. Unlike calls where you buy shares, when you buy puts, you have the option to sell shares at a specific price. People who buy puts hope the price of the stock will fall before the option expires. If the share price falls, then they make money. Either way, you may also purchase puts to protect an existing position. This would act as a form of insurance. This technique is called a protective put.

Good to know

People who buy puts hope the price of the stock will fall before the option expires. If the share price falls, then they make money.

In review, where options are concerned, investors can:

- Buy or sell calls
- Buy or sell puts

If you buy an option, you are considered a holder. If you sell options, you are considered a writer.

If you buy a call or put, you're a holder and are in no way required to take action — you have the right but not the obligation.

If you sell a call or put, you're obligated to fulfill the terms of the contract if the buyer of that option decides to exercise their option.

More terms to think about

Premium: This is the price of an option contract that the buyer of the option pays to the option seller for the right conveyed by the option contract. It's essentially the cost of the option, paid by the buyer. If you write a call on Microsoft stock and are paid $100 total by the buyer, the $100 you receive is the premium. (You don't have to give it back, even if the option expires and the buyer doesn't take any action.)

Expiration date: This is the date until when the option can be exercised. An option with an expiration date of May 31, 2022, cannot be exercised after that date — it expires, and the contract becomes null and void.

Strike price: This is the price at which the underlying asset can be bought or sold. This is the stated price per share at which the call seller is obligated to sell the underlying security. For example, you may write a call on Microsoft stock at $300 and if the price of Microsoft stock rises to $300 per share, it hits the strike price, and the option buyer may choose to exercise their option. You are required to sell the stock for $300 per share even if the share price rises higher. If the share price is higher than the strike price, the option is considered "in-the-money."

In-the-money: Any option that has intrinsic value. A call option is "in-the-money" if the underlying security is higher than the strike price of the call.

Covered call writing is a strategy based on selling options on assets you currently own. Your "cover" is the asset itself. If you have to deliver the asset, you're covered, because you already own it. From the covered call perspective, you have essentially added a new risk — the risk of losing the underlying asset — but at least you'll be happy in most cases with the price you receive for the asset.

Of course, if the stock price declines, you might not be that happy. Downside hedge is limited to the call premium. Beyond that, your downside risk exposure is there regardless.

If the holder of the option decides to exercise the option, you are "covered" from having to buy the stock in the open market and deliver it to the holder of the call option you wrote. When you sell (also called "write") a covered call, you instantly increase your investment income and cash flow. The tradeoff is that your upside is capped at the "strike" price until the option expires. (Note: The next examples doesn't include trading and commissions and is a calculated gross amount).

Covered call strategy, example one

Let's say you just bought 100 shares of Pepsi for $145. You write an options contract valid for 30 days to sell the shares at a specific price — $150, which, in this example is the "strike price." This means the buyer has the right at their discretion to buy your shares if the price hits $150 or more in the next 30 days. After the 30 days, the option contract will expire. For this option right, the buyer pays you a premium. We'll use $1.00 per share in this example.

This means you immediately earned $100 ($1.00 multiplied by 100 shares) as each options contract consists of 100 shares. As the seller, you benefited with a quick profit of $100 from the premium that you received up front. If the stock price stays under $150 for the next 30 days, the buyer won't buy your shares because it makes sense to buy it from the market directly. You still keep your $100 profit. If you continue to do this, writing multiple option contracts, you'll increase your total return on your investment as you collect your premiums.

If the stock price went up to $153 within the next 30 days, then the buyer may exercise the right to buy the shares at the strike price of $150 a share. In this case, you didn't sell your shares at the highest possible price — your shares were called away at the strike price ($150). However, someone a lot smarter than I am taught me a long time ago that you never lose money taking a profit.

Strike price

The price at which a specific options contract can be bought or sold when it's exercised.

What happens to the buyer? The buyer also benefited. Initially, the buyer spent $100 for the chance to buy your option, but the stock went up to $153 and the buyer got a deal at $150 per share. The buyer has an unrealized gain of $3 per share. If the buyer wants to sell the shares, the buyer will make a quick profit of $300 ($3 on each share multiplied by 100 shares). The buyer's total gain is $200 after factoring in the expense of paying you the premium of $100 initially.

As you can see, the option contract is mutually beneficial. The seller's main risk is that they have to sell at the agreed-upon strike price if the stock increases quickly, while the buyer's main risk is that the stock price doesn't go up, and they lose money by having paid a premium.

Covered call strategy, example two

An investor owns 100 shares of ABC stock. In the short term, they believe the stock might trade higher but not by more than 10% over its current price of $100 a share. To generate income, they decide to sell call options that have a strike price of $110 due to expire in nine months at a premium of $4 a share. Collecting this $4 premium creates a downside break-even price of $96 a share (minimized loss) and an upside cap of $114 a share (limited gain). At expiration, the following examples illustrate potential outcomes:

- ABC shares appreciate to $105, staying below the $110 strike price. The options expire worthless, and you keep the $4 premium from the sale of the options as well as the stock appreciation of $5. Your strategy outperforms sole stock ownership by a margin of 4%.

- ABC shares fall to $96, the break-even price. The options expire worthless, and you keep the $4 premium, which can be used to offset the $4 drop in the stock. Your strategy outperforms sole stock ownership by a margin of 4%.

- ABC shares appreciate to $120. The stock appreciates by $20, but since the stock price is now above the strike price, (the options are in-the-money), they are exercised at the $110 strike price, and you forfeit $10 of upside in the stock. Consequently, the stock is "called away" or sold from the account. The strategy allowed you to participate in some, but not all, of the upside.

Equity position

This refers to an investment made by a third party in a business in exchange for stock. The position may be taken by a third party for a variety of reasons, including expectation of a return. The third party may believe they can earn a generous return by buying shares in the business.

Adding covered calls to a traditional portfolio

An effective covered call strategy involves investing in high-quality companies that pay good dividends. Here, you can use a covered call strategy to supplement your dividend income. It's also a great way to increase income during market volatility. By selling a call option on the underlying equity position, you collect income and participate in any appreciation in the underlying stock up to the strike price.

Single Stock Example

Stock at $100 with call premium of $5 at strike price of $105

	Covered call total return at expiration		
Scenario 1: ABC stock is flat for the year	**+8%**	$3 from dividends + $5 from call	▲ Outperform
Scenario 2: Stock is down 12%	**-4%**	$8 cushions from dividends and call option	▲ Outperform
Scenario 3: Stock is up +16%	**+13%**	$8 from dividends and call option; plus $5 of stock appreciation up to the strike of $105	▼ Underperform in Bull Markets

This chart is hypothetical and simplified for illustrative purposes.

At expiration, if the underlying stock price is above the strike price, you must sell the underlying equity position at the strike price and forgo any additional appreciation in the equity position.

You also can buy back the option prior to expiration, which may result in a gain or a loss.

The writer of a covered call contract sells away potential upside appreciation in the stock in return for upfront premium income from the proceeds of the call option sale, which provides some downside protection. If the stock appreciates above the strike price at expiration, the covered call writer can either deliver the underlying shares to the option buyer and receive cash in the amount of the strike price or roll the call option by repurchasing the original call option and selling a new call option at a new, higher strike price and/or expiration.

Conversely, if the stock trades below the strike price at expiration, the option will expire worthless and the call writer will retain the entire amount of premium collected from selling the option.

Covered call strategies may seem complicated, but they can be written in just a minute or two. You create a covered call when you sell a call option on a stock position that you already own. You do this by selecting a strike price equal to or higher than the stock's current price. If you buy the stock position at the same time you sell the call, the strategy is known as a "buy/write."

You should consider a covered call strategy if you're an investor seeking to generate additional income from an equity position and, although bullish on the underlying stock, you feel the stock's price will not appreciate above the strike price before expiration. Let's not kid ourselves — when we write covered calls, sometimes stocks get called. You have to prepare yourself mentally for the occasional forfeiture of some upside. There are also tax consequences that you have to consider when your stock gets called.

Covered calls increase your potential return because you will always keep the option premium and will receive the dividend payout assuming the call holder doesn't exercise the call option. Covered calls do limit the maximum amount you can make on a rise in share prices, since you may have to sell the stock before it reaches its peak in value. Covered option writing limits your theoretical upside but, in the meantime, automatically adds to your income — it's a great strategy in a flat market or for investors who want to increase their income and consistent rate of return on a long-term basis.

Example: Verizon share purchase

Say you purchase 100 shares of Verizon stock for $54 per share. Your total investment (to keep the math simple, we'll leave out commissions) is $5,400.

Verizon stock pays a dividend of $2.56 per share, or approximately 4.6%, based on the current stock price. If the price of the stock rises or falls, the dividend amount won't necessarily change — unless the board of directors decides to change it — so the rate of dividend return will automatically change as the stock price fluctuates. This means that if the stock price stays flat, you'll at least get a 4.6% return on your investment, which is great, but you want a higher rate of return, so you write a covered call on the Verizon stock you own. You know that if the stock doesn't hit the strike price, you will keep the option premium, plus any dividends paid on the stock.

If the stock does hit the strike price, the option holder will most likely elect to exercise their option, but you'll still be paid the strike price and you'll keep the original option premium. When you write a covered call option, you have to be willing to sell the stock, but you'll be selling at a higher price (assuming an out-of-the-money call), and you will also profit from the option premium you were paid.

The first thing you do is consult the current options trading price chart for Verizon. Here's what a hypothetical chart and prices might look like for call options that will expire in 30 days:

Example: Verizon options trading prices

Current stock price: $54 per share (Expiration date: 30 days)

Strike price	Option premium
$50.00	$4.10
$52.50	$1.75
$54.00	$0.75 (at-the-money)
$55.00	$0.30
$56.00	$0.15
$57.00	$0.10
$60.00	$0.02

This chart is hypothetical and simplified for illustrative purposes.

As you can see, the strike price in our example goes as low as $50 per share, even though the stock is trading at $54 per share. Those options are in-the-money and could potentially be exercised right away. You would typically only sell these calls if you were bearish short-term on the stock, or you were tactically trying to exit the position.

Now let's look at the other end of the scale. An option to purchase the stock at $56 costs $0.15 per share, or $15 for 100 shares. While that's not a lot of money, the rate of return is actually fairly high. If the option isn't exercised in the next month, you keep the $15.

If you can do that 12 times without having the stock taken away by a call exercise, your annualized rate of return is 3.3%. Add that to the dividends you'll receive, and your combined annual rate of return from cash flow alone is 7.9%. From a covered call perspective, you get this return without incurring any risk — apart from giving up the right to upside appreciation above the

Get to know the Dividend Aristocrats

An effective covered call strategy involves investing in high-quality companies that pay good dividends ... and you'll learn more through examples of some Dividend Aristocrats, covered in Chapter 4.

strike due to writing those covered calls. Of course, there is always risk with any stock. If Verizon declines in value, covered calls will only hedge the downside to the extent of the premium collected. Having said that, if Verizon had jumped to $70 per share, and you're contractually obligated to sell it at $56, in that instance, it might not feel like a win.

If the option is exercised, you will have to sell the stock. If that's the case, you'll also make a profit on the higher per share price.

- Covered call: Win. √
- Dividend yield: Win. √
- Profit on higher share price: Win. √

Win-win-win!

The BXM Index

In 2002, the Chicago Board Options Exchange (CBOE) introduced the CBOE S&P 500 BuyWrite Index (BXM) as a benchmark to track the performance of a mechanical covered call strategy. The passive index was designed to show the hypothetical performance of an investment strategy that buys the S&P 500 Index and sells the nearest one-month, at-the-money call option against the underlying position. At option expiration, typically occurring on the third Friday of the month, the strategy sells a new one-month, at or slightly out-of-the-money call option (actually, the Saturday following the third Friday, but that fact is more a matter of semantics).

Downside Protection during Bear Markets
2007-2009 Downside protection during sell-offs

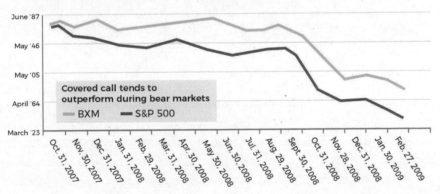

Source: CBOE

BACKSTORY:

You're not going to run across a busy highway just to pick up a nickel.

I was taught that covered calls were always the answer. Today, I operate in opposition to that concept. Many of my investing philosophies can be traced back to the inflexibility of certain investment strategies. For example, the idea that you should only own a round lot (100 shares) and that you should write covered calls on every position so you can maximize your premiums. This was a tremendous bone of contention from my perspective.

The old-time covered call writers pride themselves on how much premium they can generate. I see it differently. Whether I generated that result through dividends, covered call premiums, or market appreciation is much less important than how much money you started with and how much you have now — risk-adjusted total return is all that matters.

Another area my philosophy differs is with round lots of shares of stocks. Owning odd lots was seen as problematic to my forebearers. Here's why: Let's say you purchase 162 shares of a stock — you can only write one covered call on the 100-share position. The extra 62 shares are just wasted since you can't write a call on that 62-share lot. It's not a waste. In fact, it could very well improve the total return over time. In my eyes, the odd lot could be a good thing because if these stocks go up, you're not going to have your entire position called out, and you can get a little more of the upside with the remaining shares. I can almost see smoke coming from the ears of people who teach this business because it's counterintuitive to everything they believe.

Investing veterans tend to think that we're so good at what we do, and we're so skilled in options, that every day, in every environment, and in every single market, covered call writing is the ideal solution. I believe there are many instances in which it's actually counterproductive.

A lot of brokers in the office back in the day would sit at their desks, smoke, and play poker after 4:00 p.m. To make my point, I'd say, "You don't put all your chips in on every hand. You look at your cards and you think about it." Covered call writing should be the same way — use them when it makes sense to do so. It never makes sense to cross a busy highway to pick up a proverbial nickel.

Look at the market landscape of the position, how volatility plays into it, then decide if it's productive to write a covered call. Many times, it isn't. That's why I believe in a tactical approach to writing covered calls. It allows us to harvest volatility when it's appropriate and be smart to dial back, and stay out of the way when markets are performing well and rising tides are lifting all ships.

Even though we're probably not going to outperform the upside — there's always going to be some forfeiture since with covered calls a good stock is going to get called away from time to time — we can participate in a whole lot more of the upside if you look at it from my perspective of a tactical vs. systematic approach to covered call writing. It's like I always say: Covered calls work best when you need them the most.

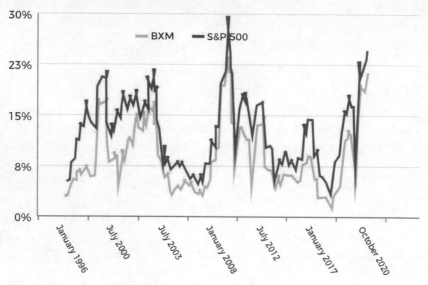

Covered call has lower volatility compared to the S&P Index
January 1996 - October 2020

Source: CBOE

Since its launch, the BXM Index strategy has generated impressive results compared to the S&P 500 Index in terms of risk mitigation and volatility reduction, providing excess relative returns during bear markets at roughly one-third less volatility than the underlying S&P 500 Index. The results are due primarily to the benchmark's conservative strategy of selling at or slightly out-of-the-money index options on 100% of the underlying equity index.

Portfolio diversification and income

When you include a covered call asset class into your portfolio, you can diversify equity and fixed income allocations in your balanced portfolio. With its lower volatility, a covered call strategy can also afford a greater risk budget for a balanced investor to allocate assets into equity investments. This would enhance the potential risk-adjusted return (whether the risk taken was worth the expected reward) for the entire portfolio with only modest adjustments to the risk profile.

Diversify interest-rate risk

Investors can enhance total yield by allocating call premium income.

Top 10 Equity Holdings	5-Year Bond Annual Yield	Annual Stock Dividend Yield	Annual Call Option Premium Yield	Total (Dividend + Call Premium Annual)
Apple	1.8%	1.7%	5.0%	6.7%
Microsoft	1.8%	2.6%	3.5%	6.1%
Walmart	1.9%	2.2%	2.5%	4.7%
Chevron	1.7%	3.8%	3.0%	6.8%
Verizon	2.1%	4.7%	3.0%	7.7%
Intel	1.0%	2.4%	5.0%	7.4%
Coca Cola	0.9%	2.9%	3.0%	5.9%
AT&T	1.9%	5.6%	3.0%	8.6%
Merck	1.9%	3.1%	4.0%	7.1%
PepsiCo	1.9%	2.7%	3.0%	5.7%
Average	**1.7%**	**3.2%**	**3.5%**	**6.7%**

This chart is hypothetical and simplified for illustrative purposes.

Additionally, a covered call strategy can help in providing current income. Investors earn the stock dividend and capture the premium income to further enhance the cash-flow component of the underlying investment.

This component is particularly attractive when utilizing the more stable larger capitalization equities with already attractive dividend yields, where the total cash flow can be further enhanced by collecting call premium income.

Income-oriented investors can help diversify the interest-rate risk associated with fixed-income investing through use of a covered call strategy. While fixed-income investments are generally inversely correlated to interest rates (i.e., losing value when rates rise), covered call writers can benefit in rising rate environments as the value of call premiums tends not to be affected as much by rising interest rate levels.

Of course, investors would be choosing equity market risk over fixed-income, duration, or price risk.

In-the-money vs. out-of-the-money

Investors use different covered call strategies depending on their goals and their outlook on the market.

The first key to writing covered calls is selecting assets that you are willing to sell for the right price. Then, decide what you feel the asset will do in the short term — that will help you choose whether to write an in-the-money or out-of-the-money call.

Let's say you own Verizon stock and are concerned shares will decrease in value. You could "lock in" a price on the stock by selling an in-the-money call. An in-the-money call is one where the asset value is currently above the strike price for that asset. As a result, the premium you receive will be high because there is a high probability that it will be called.

Option premium

This is the market price of a call option composed of the intrinsic value and time value. We'll cover intrinsic and time values in Chapter 5.

Check out the chart for Verizon on page 30 and you'll see that a call with a strike price of $52.50 is selling for $1.75 per share. If Verizon falls to $52.50, you're not out any money because you "covered" yourself by writing a covered call — $52.50 strike price plus $1.75 option premium equals $54.25 ... this is slightly higher than the current price of the stock in our hypothetical example. Of course, if the stock price declines further, you lose money, but not as much as you would have lost if you had not written the option.

On the other hand, since it's in-the-money, it's also very likely the option will be exercised, so you must be willing to let the stock go, or you shouldn't write an in-the-money covered call.

Now let's say you expect Verizon shares will stay flat. In this case, you might want to generate extra income by writing a covered call. You could write an at-the-money call, which will yield a moderate option premium and potentially increase your overall return.

Of course, if the price of Verizon shares rises, the option will probably be exercised, and you'll miss out on the future upside.

Finally, let's say you expect Verizon shares to rise by a small amount. In this case, you might write an out-of-the-money call, which is when the strike price is higher than the market value of the underlying asset. You'll receive a relatively low premium, but you'll also enjoy more of the potential appreciation in the asset value. For example, say you write a 30-day covered call on Verizon with a strike price of $57.50, you'll only get $0.10 per share in option premium, but if the stock does rise to $57.50, you'll make $3.50 per share in profit, offsetting the lower premium you received.

That's why the key is determining what you think will happen to the value of the asset and then factoring in your investment goals. If you want to sell covered calls to earn a little extra money on an asset you hope to hold on to, then in a perfect world the stock price will get very close to the strike price, without going over. That way, you keep the option premium and enjoy the gain in stock value.

If you sell covered calls to increase your guaranteed return, you'll choose a strike price and expiration date that offers the greatest return — if you lose the stock, you lose the stock, but you will have received the return you wanted regardless of losing the stock, even if the call buyer exercises their option. Not bad, right?

Here's another hypothetical example of a covered call transaction. Say you own 1,000 shares of Marathon Petroleum, an energy company based in Findlay, Ohio. The stock sells at $65 per share and the dividend is $2.32, or 3.5%. Owning 1,000 shares means each year you receive $2,320 in dividends. That sure beats a savings account.

Since you want to increase your risk-adjusted rate of return, you decide to write a covered call on your shares. Here are call option prices with an expiration date three months away:

Strike Price	Option Premium
$60.00	$7.71
$65.00	$4.20
$70.00	$2.40
$75.00	$1.19

To decide which covered call to write, first consider your goals. Let's say you want to maximize your income while capturing some upside. You could sell options with a strike price of $70. You do run the risk that the stock price will increase from $65 to $70 and you'll be forced to sell, but in the meantime, you'll receive $2.40 per share for the options, or $2,400 total.

If the stock doesn't hit $70 per share, then your earnings for three months are $2,400 plus the dividends you receive. If you were able to receive the same option price, without having to sell the stock, for four times over a 12-month period, your total return on selling covered calls would be around $9,600 — plus $2,320 in dividends. Your total annual cash flow would add up to $11,920, for an 18.3% annual return.

If the stock does hit the strike price — which it very likely could (and that's okay) — then you'll have to find another stock to buy so that you can continue to receive income or else you could simply purchase more Marathon Petroleum shares and start the covered call investment cycle all over again. In this hypothetical example, our stock would be called at $70 per share, allowing us to participate in another $5 per share of appreciation. This would add another 7.1% to the total return.

Go, Colonials!

A fun fact about the author: The Philadelphia native majored in finance at The George Washington University.

There are two important things to keep in mind here. First, you won't lose money simply from writing covered calls. Once you write the call, you receive the premium and it's yours to keep whether the stock goes up, down, or sideways. If the underlying asset value declines, you may lose money on that decline. However, assuming you wanted to hold the stock, you would've lost money regardless of whether you sold an option on that asset if you continued to hold it. The call premiums served as a modest hedge.

For example, I buy CSX stock at $32 per share and it falls to $27 per share, I've lost $5 per share. Period. If I sold a covered call, I keep that money and it actually helps to offset losses in my share value, and at least slightly reduces my total loss.

However, you can miss out on potential profits. If I buy CSX stock at $32 per share and write a covered call with a strike price of $35 and CSX goes up to $38 per share before the expiration date of the call and the option is exercised (which it most likely will be), I will have to sell the stock at $35 per share, giving me a profit of $3 per share. I will also miss out on the additional $3 per share in appreciation. Sometimes that happens.

What are the odds that CSX stock will jump from $32 to $38 in a short period of time — in, say, 30 days? The odds aren't very high, and if that does happen, I still will have made a $3 per-share profit, and I keep the option premium, which means I will have made over 10% in profits in 30 days. On an annual basis — assuming I could execute that trade 12 more times — my rate of return would total 120%. Instead of regretting the loss of additional profits, I'll happily pocket that kind of return and move on to another potentially profitable covered call investment.

Buying individual stocks is inherently risky. Experts often say you should diversify your portfolio, and I agree. Buying individual stocks, unless you have substantial sums to invest and can afford to buy shares in a variety of companies, makes it tough for the average investor to build a diversified investment portfolio and minimize the risk of exposure to an under-performing market investment sector or specific stock risk. If you can't build a diversified portfolio of your own, you could consider writing covered calls on exchange-traded funds — diversification is a given when you choose the right funds.

Now that you understand the basics of covered calls, let's look at the benefits and risks of this investment strategy. My goal is for you to understand the upside and potential downside, and make the smartest decisions possible.

Benefits and risks of covered calls

Writing covered calls on exchange-traded funds (ETFs) has the potential to generate double-digit annual rates of return through the combination of dividends, option premiums, and capital appreciation. There's a degree of risk with all options trading, but writing covered calls limits your risk to merely capping your upside on a bullish move in the stock and is a great way to protect from market downturns and generate solid returns in almost any market.

At the same time, every investment strategy involves both benefits and potential risks — so let's look at both, focusing on the positives and nega-

BACKSTORY:

I took those career aptitude tests, and they typically had me ending up in education.

If you think about it, that's what I do — teach. As far back as high school, I've never thought of doing anything else. I can't even imagine what that would be like.

tives of writing covered calls on ETFs.

Benefits of covered calls

Generate additional income or return. Covered calls have the potential to generate a steady stream of income in flat to rising markets. Regardless of changes in the market or economy, you keep the premiums (income earned) from any covered calls you write. You receive an upfront premium from the sale of the option. Selling options allows the owner of the underlying security to collect both dividend distributions and premium income from the call option.

Receive income almost immediately. When you write a covered call, the premium is credited to your account within a day or so, where you can then reinvest it or use it for your monthly household cash flow. Since you don't have to worry about paying the premium back, you can spend it any way you wish.

How to choose your advisor

In Chapter 7, you'll learn about the primary types of financial advisors and how to find the right fit for your unique needs.

Predictably generate guaranteed rates of return. With covered calls, you will know the initial and maximum rate of return you can expect if your option is used when you write the covered call.

Reduce risk. If the value of your ETF falls, writing a covered call and receiving the premium helps to buffer the total loss in your investment.

Receive dividends until you sell the ETF. When you write a covered call on an ETF, you give another person the right to purchase your shares under specific conditions. In the meantime, you receive any cash dividends distributed by the fund.

Convenient trading. Covered calls are traded on the open markets. You can buy and sell options just like you sell individual stocks or ETFs. You can use a broker or handle your own trades online.

Portfolio diversification. ETFs are available for all major stock indices, including the Dow, the S&P 500, and the NASDAQ Composite index. You can buy ETFs for large U.S. companies, small companies, real estate investment trusts (REIT), international stocks, bonds, and even commodities. Almost every asset class is represented by an ETF.

Reduced downside risk. Investors often consider the sale of the call option as a form of downside protection. The amount of downside protection is equal to the upfront call premium received. The upfront premium from the sale of the call option can be used to partially offset a decline in price.

Stock ownership benefits. Unless the stock is called away, you maintain all the benefits of stock ownership, such as dividend and voting rights.

Volatility reduction. Equity investors are exposed to a great deal of volatility within portfolios. Although committed to the growth prospects of the equity asset class, many investors may be willing to trade this volatility for greater return consistency.

Risks of covered calls

Requires an underlying investment in stocks. ETFs are typically stock-market-based investments (unless you purchase, for example, a fixed-income or commodities-based fund.) If the market dips, the value of your ETF is likely to decrease, as well. On the flip side, writing covered calls does provide some amount of protection against losses since premiums can offset some or all of the loss in value of an underlying ETF. In short, if you plan to purchase shares of an ETF, writing covered calls automatically reduces your level of risk, even if only by a small amount.

Upside gains might be limited. If the value of an ETF exceeds the strike price, the option may be exercised by the buyer and the shares will be sold. If the value continues to rise, you will miss out on those gains since you will no longer own shares in the ETF. In some cases, you may have been better off not selling covered calls, especially if the market explodes upward. On the other hand, you will be able to predict your rate of return when you write the covered call, so you enjoy the benefit of making an informed decision about the level of return you hope to receive. The biggest risk that you have with covered calls is that you miss out on a stock's potential appreciation after a certain point because covered calls are inherently fiscally conservative strategies geared toward providing a modest hedge against loss.

Covered calls can be exercised at any time. While options are typically exercised at the expiration date, the holder of the option is entitled to exercise their rights at any time up to the expiration date. You could lose the ETF shares before you think you will, but if that happens, you will also immediately be paid the strike price for those shares. In this scenario, while you lost the shares, you also received money to reinvest elsewhere so you can continue to seek high rates of return.

Trading could be thin. Options are generally traded less widely than normal stocks are. Plus, options for some stocks are more widely traded than others, and options for some ETFs are less widely traded than others — but some ETFs have extremely active option trading. On thinly traded ETF options, the difference between the "bid" (what someone will pay) and the "ask" (what you want to receive) could be fairly large. A broker can help you place a limit order (specifying the terms of your call pricing) to ensure that your calls are sold at a price you're comfortable with.

Premium amounts vary as the market varies. When the market is volatile, option prices tend to be higher. When the market is stable, option prices tend to be lower. Predictability — or at least perceived predictability — tends to create lower prices. The premium amounts you receive for options of a particular ETF may vary over time, and your rate of return could increase or decrease as you write subsequent covered calls. But keep in mind, once you write a covered call, your rate of return for that option is guaranteed — money in your pocket is guaranteed income.

Commissions may vary. To execute a trade, whether in stocks, ETFs, options, or covered calls on ETFs, you may need to pay a commission to the executing firm or broker. Commission rates vary widely — make sure you find a brokerage that offers the services you need at a price you feel is reasonable for those services.

When can you trade options?

Now that you know the general benefits and risks of writing covered calls on ETFs, you'll want to take note of the times that you can trade options on exchanges. As with individual stocks, regular market hours (9:30 a.m. – 4:00 p.m. EST) apply to most ETFs and narrow-based index options, where broad-based index and some ETF options have an extra 15-minute trade window until 4:15 p.m. EST. Options are open for trading on a given day once their underlying security has started trading.

Remember, a covered call strategy can make a huge difference to qualified accounts, helping you grow and safeguard your money for retirement and other long-term goals. Qualified accounts often contain an individual's life savings and retirement funds from their 401(k) and IRA accounts.

With a covered call strategy, you don't have to pay taxes on the option premiums collected, dividends collected, or on stocks bought and sold for a gain. There are no constraints on selling. This differs greatly from non-qualified accounts where low-cost basis positions are often not sold because taxes would be recognized. You have more flexibility and choices when you employ a covered call strategy for your qualified account.

Covered calls are also advantageous in qualified accounts because there are no taxes on the covered calls, the dividends, or when you buy or sell stocks from your account. All your gains, dividends, and option premiums compile on a tax-deferred basis.

If you're still wondering if a covered call strategy is suitable for you, consider this: In my opinion, any individual who has $250,000 or more to invest is in a good position to write covered calls on a diversified portfolio of dividend-paying stocks. For smaller amounts, it might make more sense to use ETFs. If appropriate, you can roll over your individual retirement accounts, such as your 401(k) plan from your employer (maximum contribution of $20,500 per year as of 2022), and you can diversify your portfolio to include covered calls, dividends, and options.

No, no, no

In qualified accounts, you don't have to pay taxes on the option premiums collected, dividends collected, or on stocks bought and sold for a gain.

This makes a tremendous difference over time, especially with accounts of $500,000 - $1 million. The covered call strategy is also suitable for trusts, endowments, and larger organizations with 401(k) accounts to manage. Please be sure to check with your tax, accounting, and financial planning professionals before engaging in any new investment strategy — including covered call writing.

You need to know exactly what you're getting into. I'm not an accountant, and you don't want to rely soley on my brief sentence or two about taxes.

I know this is a lot of information to take in, but you're doing great — keep powering through!

Key takeaway

Covered calls work best when we need them to most. They limit your risk to merely capping your upside on a bullish move in the stock and are a great way to protect from market volatility while generating solid returns in almost any market.

"It is a mistake to try to look too far ahead. The chain of destiny can only be grasped one link at a time."

- Sir Winston Churchill, British Prime Minister

T he one way to receive frequent cash payouts through equity investments is through businesses that pay regular dividends. While this may seem like abrupt opening dialogue for this chapter, it's actually the steadiest investing advice that any of us could hope for.

Far too often when it comes to the stock market and investing, the public prefers drama and publicized promotions over stocks that provide steady sales and a rising dividend yield. There's no doubt the talking heads can be attention-grabbing and fun to watch, while tracking stocks can be yawn-inducing. Nevertheless, companies that are just starting out are rarely the best long-term investments for the income-oriented investor. In fact, as many as 80% of all new businesses will fail within the first five years. A company that provides regular payouts has to exercise fiscal discipline, and this can take years. The main point: History shows that dividend-paying stocks are less risky and produce more income than other stocks.

A dividend stock pays stockholders a dividend in cash or shares. Dividend-paying companies distribute part of their profits every quarter or every month to shareholders and then invest the remaining profits into the company to propel growth. A payout ratio is the percentage of total profits that a company pays out in dividends to shareholders. Companies that pay dividends need to have stable cash flow to do so, with enough profits beyond meeting their obligations and debts to pay shareholders regular dividends. This is why high-quality, dividend-paying stocks tend to hold up better than non-dividend paying stocks, even during market declines. This is because they are mature, stable, and derived from highly profitable companies that have plenty of cash and long-term endurance.

Dividend stocks are an appealing choice for individual income-oriented investors because they offer the potential for share-price appreciation and the ability to receive profits through cash payments (i.e., dividends) without selling shares. While stock prices go up and down every day, dividends tend to be a bit more stable.

Trust the process

You never want to be the investor who missed out on the market's average 8+% annual return because you moved investments at the wrong time ... so be aware of listening to too many talking heads and getting spooked.

Far too often, individual investors engage in speculative behavior when they see markets moving against their portfolios or ramping up without their direct involvement. That impulse to jump back and forth becomes even more stressful when markets reverse as quickly as they changed in the first place.

The result? You guessed it, portfolios lose significant value and the investors who jump around tend to fare far worse than those who stayed the course and retained their holdings longer. You never want to be the investor who misses out on the market's average 8+% annual return because you moved investments at the wrong time.

In some respects, investing in stocks without dividends could be considered speculative because they don't offer cash value outside of selling the stock outright. In the early years of the stock market and to the middle of the twentieth century, most stocks in the United States paid dividends. This was the common practice of the old-world dividend stocks on the New York Stock Exchange (NYSE). Individual investors could rely on dividends as a regular source of income. Fast forward, though, to the 1980s and 1990s, and you see a shift toward no dividends at all, with the rise of the NASDAQ and the tech boom. This is apparent today, with 25% of stocks in the NASDAQ Composite Index (689 of the 2,726 companies) paying a dividend. As of 2021, the nominal payment of less than 1.0% yield was offered by 203 stocks in the S&P 500. Altogether, this represents 56% of the S&P 500 market capitalization.

In the last few decades, the United States has moved away from having a stock market with regular, long-term profit streams. It now operates more like a trading market where stocks do not offer any cash value. Even among the S&P 500 Index, historically known for its dividend-oriented U.S.-listed stocks, the percentage of companies offering dividends fell from 95% in 1965 to 78% in 2021.

Industries in which many of these non-dividend stocks co-exist, such as information technology, Alphabet (GOOGL), and publicly traded large conglomerates such as Berkshire Hathaway (BRK.A), are often well-established, stable, and profitable. Some others pay nominal dividends, and we don't consider them suitable for our income-oriented investment objectives.

Trading in non-dividend securities has become so commonplace that dividend investing has been pushed back. In many ways, this is antithetical to what's best for investors seeking the powerful combination of growth in value and steady income because the point of investing is to make money and generate cash flow.

Search engine

Known around the world, Google abruptly renamed itself Alphabet in 2015, making Google a subsidiary. As a parent company, Alphabet allowed Google to expand into domains outside of Internet search and advertising to become a technology conglomerate.

Consider GOOGL, the stock of a reputable and well-established company, now reorganized as one of several companies under the Alphabet umbrella of companies. Alphabet was created through a corporate restructuring of Google on October 2, 2015. The share price of GOOGL has steadily climbed, and as of September 30, 2021, was $2,819.58. In 2010, prior to the restructuring, Google's stock was valued at over $600 already. Google stock does not offer any dividend payout — it's based purely on the mentality of buy, sell, and reposition. For the smaller group of expe-

BACKSTORY:

Quality never goes out of style.

During 1999, when the tech bubble was in its heyday, companies that investors had never heard of were appreciating exponentially. This gave speculators the opportunity to make 100% returns in as little as one week. The experience of the tech bubble certainly helped form a lasting memory in my mind — both of the frustration of day-traders wanting to make those types of returns, and the sadness that inevitably came to those who went down with the ship when the tech market corrected.

Going through this time in the industry helped form one of our core philosophies: Know what you own when it comes to companies to invest in. It was also important to cover companies in our covered call strategy that didn't have the possibility of dot-com meteoric gains. That formulated our thesis for tactical covered call writing and allowed us to dial back the call writing in instances and periods of low volatility.

Prior to the correction, there was a wave of criticism against Warren Buffet because he wouldn't look at the skyrocketing tech companies as viable investments, because they weren't. They were speculations. I remember talking heads and pundits in the Wall Street Journal who were putting Buffet out to pasture. At the same time, in the office, phones were constantly ringing and trades were very active. But, it was Buffet who got the last laugh in February 2000 when the bubble burst. And, in the office then, it was so quiet that I could imagine tumbleweeds rolling across my desk. It was a valuable lesson to stick with high-quality companies for stock selection.

rienced day traders who know how to cash in on this casino-style trading that has become popular in mainstream culture, some profit can be made. Of course, a buy-and-hold investor in Google has also done really, really well. What you're missing is any cash payout of this accrued value. You've only generated cash when the stock is sold.

The fact remains that the stock doesn't offer a dividend payout and its value is tied only to its sale. The stock market crashes of 2020 and 2008 (and the previously during the dot-com bust) showed that tech stocks are volatile, and stocks cannot always be cashed out for their trading value or what you bought them for. The reality is that if you don't receive an income stream from your stocks, then you're dependent on a buyer for any cash value from your stock purchase, and only when you sell.

For individuals who love to take risks, expendable cash and enjoyment of daily swings are key. It's similar to playing cards with experienced, professional card players, with the rest of the table losing out. An investment environment like this is littered with anxiety, stress, turnover, high fees, complex taxes, and lower returns. We live in a time where serious investing has been pushed to the sidelines, while day traders chase ticker prices.

Despite the 2020 COVID crash, 2008 financial meltdown, and the busted tech bubble, most investors still think of stocks first and dividends second, or not at all.

These speculators fail to pay attention to an important component of total return — dividends. Careful investment in a high-yielding, dividend-growing strategy can lead to long-term success.

It holds true

John Burr Williams said it perfectly in his book, *The Theory of Investment Value* (1938): "Stock is worth the present value of all the dividends ever to be paid upon it, no more, no less. Present earnings, outlook, financial condition, and capitalization should bear upon the price of a stock only as they assist buyers and sellers in estimating future dividends."

How dividends influence returns

Since 1926, approximately 32% of market returns have come from dividends. When you look at the data, 4.7% of the 8.7% total return of the stock market before 1957 — pre-S&P 500 Index days — came from dividends, according to data from Robert Schiller's database at Yale University. Historically, dividend-paying equities also have provided higher cumulative returns with lower levels of volatility when compared to non-dividend paying equities over longer holding periods.

Over the long term, the value of companies goes up because their distributable profits go up. Dividends dominate total returns, which means it makes sense to invest in them. In fact, in the book *Security Analysis* (1934), value investors Benjamin Graham and David L. Dodd assert that dividends are the main component of long-term total return.

In the 1930s and 1940s, there was little difference between value investing and dividend investing. This is where both Graham and Dodd emphasized the importance of dividends as a tangible expression of a successful value approach: "The outside, or public, shareholder gets no tangible, realizable benefit from his investment except by way of dividends received thereon or through an increase in the marketplace. The latter in turn is usually dependent upon the former.

Increased value

Dividends don't cause successful investing, but they are the manifestation of successful investing when companies are able to distribute company profits.

"Thus, it is an accepted tenet of financial theory that the present value of any preferred or common stock issue, and any other investment assumed to have no maturity or repayment date for its principal, is the sum of the present values of all the future expectable dividends or interest payments therefrom."

They insist that investors should ask for adequate dividends.

It's important to know that every company has its own dividend policy that reflects the preferences of the board of directors and shareholders. There are other factors that can influence dividend payments and policies, such as the Jobs and Growth Tax Relief Reconciliation Act of 2003 that decreased the maximum tax rate on dividends from 39.6% to 15%. Many companies in the S&P 500 Index chose to then boost dividend payments.

The more a company raises its dividend, the more the business value increases as long as that dividend growth is a result of increasing earnings.

When a company is doing well and increases its profits, it can provide

S&P 500 total return: Dividends vs. capital appreciation

Average annualized returns

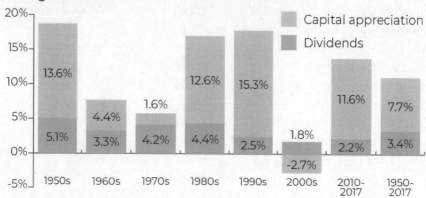

Legend:
- Capital appreciation
- Dividends

Decade	Capital appreciation	Dividends
1950s	13.6%	5.1%
1960s	4.4%	3.3%
1970s	1.6%	4.2%
1980s	12.6%	4.4%
1990s	15.3%	2.5%
2000s	-2.7%	1.8%
2010-2017	11.6%	2.2%
1950-2017	7.7%	3.4%

Asset class yields

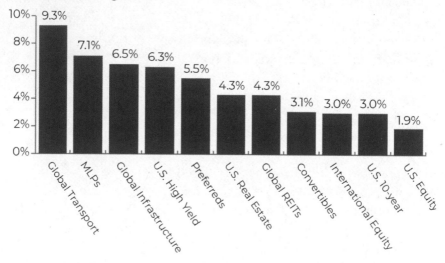

Asset class	Yield
Global Transport	9.3%
MLPs	7.1%
Global Infrastructure	6.5%
U.S. High Yield	6.3%
Preferreds	5.5%
U.S. Real Estate	4.3%
Global REITs	4.3%
Convertibles	3.1%
International Equity	3.0%
U.S. 10-year	3.0%
U.S. Equity	1.9%

Source: FactSet, Standard & Poor's, J.P. Morgan Asset Management; (Top) Ibbotson; (Bottom) Alerian, BAML, Barclays, Bloomberg, Clarkson, Drewry Maritime Consultants, Federal Reserve, FTSE, MSCI, NCREIF. Dividend vs.capital appreciation returns are through 12/31/17. Yields are as of 6/30/18, except Global Transport, Global Infrastructure and U.S. Real Estate (3/31/18). Yields for each of the sub-vessel types above are calculated and respectiveweightings are applied to each of the sub-sectors to arrive at the current levered yields for Global Transportation;MLPs: Alerian MLP; Preferreds: BAML Hybrid Preferred Securities; U.S. High Yield: Bloomberg US Aggregate Corporate High Yield; U.S. Equity: MSCIUSA. Guide to the Markets – U.S. Data are as of July 31, 2018.

more cash distributions to the owners of the company. Dividends don't cause successful investing, but they're the manifestation of successful investing when companies are able to distribute corporate profits. Large, established companies don't sit on profits. Instead, they distribute earnings to the owners of the company. Otherwise, they could lose their owners and investors.

While there are many companies in tech and other industries that don't offer dividend payments but have successfully grown and expanded their businesses and profits, they don't offer you, the individual investor, any return on your investment unless you sell their stock. Dividends, on the other hand, provide reliable, indisputable cash flow. The dividend enhances long-term total return by combining the basic yield and dividend growth, adding a cash distribution to the growth in market value.

Yield

A yield is the return a company gives back to investors for investing in a stock, bond, or other security. It's a return measure for an investment over a set period of time. expressed as a percentage.

Immediate cash

Dividend stocks provide investors with a reliable income, unlike non-dividend stocks. This is particularly important for the baby boomer population who are retiring in increasing numbers and need enough retirement income to pay their monthly bills and medical expenses for a long and healthy retirement. When you have a high-yielding, dividend-paying portfolio, you may be able to generate enough cash flow to cover expenses without having to sell your stock investments.

Dividends offer you quarterly cash income (like a regular paycheck). This could be cash that you use to pay your monthly utilities, rent or mortgage, grocery bills, and more. Now, if you have invested in a dividend stock that gives you a higher yield (3+%, for example), you would have more money to spend per month from your dividend income.

This example uses round figures and excludes taxes and fees:

If you need $2,000 a month as a retiree for your monthly expenses, then you would need a stock market portfolio of $1,200,000 to generate this cash monthly at a 2.0% yield. This would allow you to use your interest and not consume the principal. However, if you had a dividend-focused portfolio with a 3.5% yield, the same monthly requirement can be met with about $700,000 in assets.

While receiving income from equities may be new to you, it's still a viable way to bring in reliable income. Given that regular income from money market funds, CDs, corporate bonds, and government securities have declined significantly in value, while the cost of living and medical expenses has continued to climb, retirees who can find alternate sources of income with regular cash flows should be much better off.

I particularly like stocks that constantly raise their dividends. As important as dividend growth is in our strategy, it's just as important, if not more so, that the companies we own are increasing their dividends for the right reason: earnings growth.

Bulls and bears

A bull market occurs when securities are on the rise, while a bear market occurs when securities fall for a sustained period of time.

It's like my wife, JoAnna, and I teach our son, Jack: Anyone can buy whatever they want. Armed with a credit card, we can go to the mall and purchase just about anything. However, that doesn't mean that we can necessarily afford it. Considering the rates credit card companies charge, consumer debt isn't something I want to encourage.

It's no different with publicly traded companies. They need to have fiscal responsibility. Any company can leverage their business to increase a dividend. We want to invest in corporations that can afford their dividend growth.

Like any other investment, dividend stocks have benefits and risks, because when you receive a dividend, you're essentially collecting cash flow on money you have invested in a company.

Dividend benefits

Regular, passive income. Dividends provide a steady stream of passive income that you can reinvest or spend. This regular income makes dividend-stock investing very appealing to retirees seeking supplemental cash flow.

Stocks in good companies trend higher over time.

Early in my career, I would point to the stock market chart that everyone had on the wall behind their desk — it would go up from bottom-left to top-right. Corrections and fluctuations happen in between, of course, but for the most part if you own stock in good companies, they tend to trend higher over time.

Stable companies. Companies that pay dividends tend to be more stable than startups that are rapidly consuming all their profits to fuel growth. A company needs to reach a level of sustainable success before its board of directors will vote to pay out dividends. Paying out dividends requires accountability to shareholders, and management is also less likely to take large risks.

Lowered risk with two ways to profit. In many cases, dividends have a lower risk-to-reward ratio because they offer investors two ways to get a return on their investment: 1) share-price appreciation and, 2) dividend cash payments. There's less volatility in the share price. A stock that has lower volatility has smaller share price declines when the market plummets. Of course, lower volatility stocks will still go down during corrections. They're not immune to the whims of the market.

Retain stock ownership while collecting profits. You can continue to own your stocks while you collect a share of profits. By far, one of the most frustrating aspects of owning shares in a company that doesn't pay dividends is that you have to sell your shares to access profits because those profits are tied completely to the stock price.

Receive cash to buy more shares. You can purchase new shares simply by reinvesting part or all of your dividends, and you can even automatically reinvest your shares with some programs. When you buy shares in a company that doesn't pay dividends, you own the number of shares you bought. If you want more shares, you have to pay to acquire more.

Positive return in bear markets. In a bear market, when share prices drop, or in range-bound flat markets, companies that pay dividends continue to pay dividends. These payments can offset some of the decline in share price and over time can even provide a positive return. At the very least, you get paid while you wait for better times to return.

Four times

Tradition still carries a great deal of weight, and it has become the norm for most regular corporations to pay dividends on a quarterly basis. Many well-known dividend-paying companies, such as Coca-Cola and Johnson & Johnson, pay dividends on a quarterly basis.

Hedge against inflation. Dividends can offset inflation-based earnings loss. In fact, companies that charge more for their products, contributing to inflation, also tend to earn more and pay out larger dividends.

Dividend risks

Drop in share prices. Whether the company pays dividends or not, there can be a drop in share prices. In the worst-case scenario, the company goes bankrupt before you have the opportunity to sell your shares.

Companies trim or slash dividend payments. Companies are not required by law to pay dividends or to increase payments. Unlike bonds, companies don't go into default if they don't pay interest. Companies can cut and even remove dividends at any time. As we'll learn in chapter 8, if this happens, I sell the stock.

Know the dates

As an extended part of our dividend benefits overview, it's important to understand when they're paid out. The following list of dates can help you determine when you'll receive a dividend stock's next dividend payment:

Trade date. This refers to the date that you actually buy the stock.

Settlement date. For stocks, the settlement date is three business days after the trade date, so a trade that took place on Monday would typically settle on Wednesday. This represents the day that the purchase becomes finalized and you become a "shareholder of record" on the company's books. Think of the settlement date like the closing date of a real estate transaction.

Ex-dividend date. This is the first day a stock trades without its dividend. If you buy shares before the ex-dividend date, you are entitled to that dividend payment. If you purchase the shares on or after this date, you won't get paid until the next dividend cycle.

Record date. This date occurs two business days after the ex-dividend date and is the date the company determines who gets a dividend and who doesn't. This ensures that everyone who completed a trade before the ex-dividend date becomes a shareholder of record on or before the record date.

Pay date. This is the date when the dividend is paid to shareholders.

Dow Jones, S&P 500, and NASDAQ

Dividend stock options are available on the major stock market indices, including Dow Jones, S&P, and the NASDAQ. The S&P 500 (SPX) is a price-return index and, therefore, dividends aren't incorporated into the total index value. Instead, dividends affect the price of the constituent stocks, so they influence the individual stock index value.

Since the dividends are known ahead of time or can be estimated, this figure is factored into the futures price by the market. Dividend stocks of the Dow 30 are considered some of the most attractive options because they're usually more mature blue-chip companies.

S&P 500's Dividend Aristocrats

Large-cap stock

The stocks of any publicly traded company valued at more than $10 billion. Sometimes called big-cap stocks, large-cap stocks are often thought of as the stalwarts (or blue chips) of the stock market.

While they're known primarily for their steady payout growth, as an investment class, the Dividend Aristocrats have also consistently performed well from a total return perspective over the long term. There are 65 companies on the 2021 Dividend Aristocrats list.

To be a Dividend Aristocrat, a company must meet strict requirements. Among them, the company must:

• Be a member of the S&P 500 index.

• Have a minimum of one dividend increase annually for at least the last 25 years.

• Be worth $3 billion at the time of each quarterly rebalancing.

Dividend Aristocrats can be found in many industry sectors. They're all large-cap, blue-chip companies. Dividend Aristocrats have maintained their dividend increases through market changes with a resilient business model and consistent earnings growth.

In the decade ending in 2019, the S&P 500's annualized return was 13.57%. For the same period, the Dividend Aristocrats Index had an annualized 14.75% return, 1.18% higher than the market. Dividends have also accounted for approximately 20% of the market's total return. As of September 30, 2021, the top three sectors by weight in the Dividend

The 2021 List of Dividend Aristocrats (65)

Consumer staples
- Archer-Daniels-Midland (ADM)
- Brown-Forman Corporation (BF-B)
- The Clorox Company (CLX)
- The Coca-Cola Company (KO)
- Colgate-Palmolive (CL)
- Hormel Foods (HRL)
- Kimberly Clark (KMB)
- McCormick & Company (MKC)
- PepsiCo (PEP)
- Procter & Gamble (PG)
- Sysco (SYY)
- Walgreens Boots Alliance (WBA)
- Wal-Mart (WMT)

Industrials
- 3M (MMM)
- A.O. Smith (AOS)
- Caterpillar (CAT)
- Cintas Corp. (CTAS)
- Dover (DOV)
- Emerson Electric (EMR)
- Expeditors International of Washington (EXPD)
- General Dynamics (GD)
- Illinois Tool Works (ITW)
- Pentair (PNR)
- Roper Technologies (ROP)
- Stanley Black & Decker (SWK)
- W.W. Grainger (GWW)

Healthcare
- Abbott Laboratories (ABT)
- AbbVie (ABBV)
- Becton, Dickinson & Co. (BDX)
- Cardinal Health (CAH)
- Johnson & Johnson (JNJ)
- Medtronic (MDT)
- West Pharma. Services (WST)

Consumer discretionary
- Genuine Parts Company (GPC)
- Leggett & Platt (LEG)
- Lowe's (LOW)
- McDonald's (MCD)
- Target (TGT)
- V.F. Corporation (VFC)

Financials
- Aflac (AFL)
- Chubb (CB)
- Cincinnati Financial (CINF)
- Franklin Resources (BEN)
- People's United Financial (PBCT)
- S&P Global (SPGI)
- T. Rowe Price Group (TROW)

Materials
- Air Products and Chemicals (APD)
- Albemarle Corp. (ALB)
- Amcor PLC (AMCR)
- Ecolab (ECL)
- Linde (LIN)
- Nucor (NUE)
- PPG Industries (PPG)
- Sherwin-Williams (SHW)

Energy
- Chevron (CVX)
- ExxonMobil (XOM)

Information technology
- Automatic Data Processing (ADP)
- Intnl. Business Machines (IBM)

Real estate
- Essex Property Trust Inc. (ESS)
- Federal Realty Investment Trust (FRT)
- Realty Income Corp. (O)

Communications services
- AT&T (T)

Utilities
- Atmos Energy Corp. (ATO)
- Consolidated Edison (ED)
- NextEra Energy Inc. (NEE)

Historical Performance

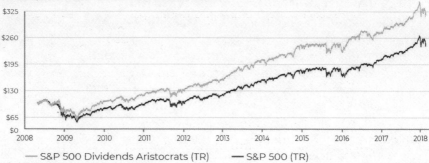

— S&P 500 Dividends Aristocrats (TR)   — S&P 500 (TR)

Source: Standard and Poor's

Aristocrats are consumer staples, industrials, and materials. The weight of these sectors in the S&P 500 vs. the Dividend Aristocrats is shown here for comparison.

	S&P 500	**Dividend Aristocrats**
Consumer Staples	5.8%	20%
Industrials	8%	19.3%
Materials	2.5%	12.6%

The first list of Dividend Aristocrats was published in 1989. There were 26 companies on that inaugural list, and as of 2021, there are 65. Seven remain from that original list, among them Coca-Cola Company (KO), Johnson & Johnson (JNJ), and Proctor and Gamble (PG). These companies have increased their dividend for 59, 59, and 64 consecutive years, respectively. The number of companies on the list had previously peaked in 2001, with 64 companies qualifying. The longest dividend growth streak of any Dividend Aristocrat is tied at 65 consecutive years between Dover Corp. (DOV) and Genuine Parts Co. (GPC).

The number of companies on the list tends to coincide with significant bear markets. For example, the initial list of just 26 companies was published 25 years following the down years in 1973-1974. That tough economy forced many companies to freeze or drop dividends, disqualifying them from the original list 25 years later. Likewise, the list had high numbers in 2001 at 64, and 60 in 2008 — the recessions that followed those peaks once again forced numerous Dividend Aristocrats off the list. We saw this happen during the COVID crash of 2020, with 65 companies on the list. During the pandemic, several companies, such as Ross Stores (ROSS) and Helmerich & Payne (HP), were forced to cut or eliminate their dividends. Unlike previous crashes, however, those removed were replaced by companies such as IBM (IBM) and NextEra Energy (NEE), resulting in 65 companies still on the list.

The 2021 list of Dividend Aristocrats is primarily composed of companies in the consumer staple (20%), industrial (19.3%), and materials (12.6%) sectors. Financial and consumer discretionary companies also represent more than 10% each on the list. Telecoms, utilities, and information technology companies are the least represented, each accounting for about 2% of the list.

To increase dividends for 25+ years is a significant achievement for any company. Only 13% of the S&P 500 qualify at this level today. To achieve such a feat, a company must be consistent and resilient with significant competitive advantages and excellent capital allocation. These factors contribute to strong fundamental performance and the dividend strength reflects this performance.

The average return on assets among Dividend Aristocrats is 8% as of September 30, 2021, 20% higher than the broader average on the S&P 500. Nineteen of the Dividend Aristocrats have the largest market cap in their industries and 37 place in the top three. In terms of stock price performance, until 2019 and 2020, the Dividend Aristocrats have outperformed the S&P 500 on a total return basis, which includes reinvested dividends. However, with Dividend Aristocrat outsiders such as Alphabet, Tesla, Meta (previously Facebook), Amazon, and Apple leading the charge over the past few years, the Aristocrats have now underperformed the S&P 500 for the most recent timeframe for the period ending September 2021.

Common stock and preferred stock

Common stock is the most common type of stock issued by companies, meaning it offers dividends to common stock owners from company profits. The company's board of directors decides whether the company pays dividends now, and determines the amount of payment. The payment is usually in the form of cash or stock. Common stock can also appreciate over time through capital appreciation, where the return and principal value of stocks fluctuate with changes in market conditions (hopefully to the upside).

Preferred stock is usually considered less volatile than common stock, but also has less potential for growth in market value. Preferred stockholders don't have voting rights, like common stockholders do, but they have a greater claim to the company's assets. Additionally, preferred stock shareholders receive their dividends before common stockholders do, and usually have higher payments. While common stockholders have variable dividend payments, preferred stock shareholders receive fixed dividend payments regularly for a specified period. Fixed dividends depend upon the company's ability to pay as promised. If a company declares bankruptcy, preferred stockholders are paid first, before common stockholders.

Both common stock and preferred stock have their own advantages. When you consider which type may be suitable for you, it's important to assess your financial situation, time frame, and investment goals. It's always a good idea to consult qualified financial planners and tax consultants.

Now you've gained knowledge about dividends, what they are, what type of companies provide them, and some historical context. You also understand why dividends are an essential part of investing.

Key takeaway

Careful investment in a high-yielding, dividend-growing strategy can produce solid, risk-adjusted returns over time. What's more, dividends offer consistent cash income like regular paychecks.

"The most important quality for an investor is temperament, not intellect."

- Warren Buffett, American business magnate, investor, philanthropist, chairman and CEO of Berkshire Hathaway

Now that you've learned the essentials of both a covered call strategy and dividend investing, and you understand how to use the stock market to tap into distributed cash flows with some downside protection, it's time to look at how to put it all together.

Investing in a high-quality dividend strategy and utilizing covered calls on both dividend stocks and ETFs can help you achieve long-term high performance in the market and protect your investments over time.

Whether you do this yourself or hire a professional, it's important to have a strategy and a disciplined approach to investing. You'll also need to research current data to make the most informed decisions. Investment decisions should be guided by a disciplined, risk-aware strategy that seeks to add value in all market environments. When buying or selling options, use a strategy that is based on your investment goals while still protecting your investment value.

Let's start with covered calls, followed by dividends.

Creating your call strategy

Here are four essential steps for crafting your covered call strategy:

1. Find a stock that you view as short-term neutral to slightly bullish. This could be a stock you already own or a stock you have a long-term bullish view on (you think it will go higher). In many cases, the time to sell covered calls is once the equity position has begun to move in your favor.

2. Determine a price you're comfortable with for your stock. If you're called, then your position will be sold at the strike price of the call. Are you happy with the return from selling your stock at that price? If your answer is yes, then consider the covered call strategy.

3. Determine the expiration date. The advantage of choosing a closer expiration is that if the call expires worthless, you can sell another — assuming your viewpoint hasn't changed.

4. Consider the overall market. When establishing a covered call, consider the market projections between now and the expiration date you set.

Know your options

Liquid option chains list all available options contracts for a particular security.

If you think the market will rise significantly, you probably don't want to limit your upside participation by selling a call. A covered call strategy is ideal for when you're neutral to slightly bullish on the overall market and the underlying stock.

Writing covered calls on ETFs

In this next segment, I focus on exchange-traded funds. My preference is to use individual stocks, but we have to recognize the amount of money required to build a diversified equity portfolio. As we discussed, it takes $200,000 - $300,000 to do it right. New investors don't always have that type of initial investment, so let's talk about ETFs for now.

ETFs are available in almost every industry. It's important that you choose a variety of ETFs across industries with liquid option chains.

We've covered the basics and the underlying principles of how you can build real wealth while minimizing risk through writing covered calls on ETFs — so, let's put what you've learned into practice. Keep in mind that we'll focus on writing covered calls on exchange-traded funds here. You will own the underlying shares of the ETFs you write options on. You won't sell naked calls (selling call options without owning the underlying asset), and as a result, won't face unlimited risk.

Here are the three essential steps you'll learn:

- How to select the right ETFs for your goals and your willingness to take on risk.
- How to determine the right terms for the option contracts you write.
- How to make the right trades.

Rinse and repeat these three steps to begin seeing the real accumulation of your wealth.

How to select the appropriate ETFs

There are more than 7,600 exchange-traded funds available, representing about $7.7 trillion, and this number is continuing to grow because ETFs are popular with institutional and individual investors. The good news is that the same problem that creates abundance also creates opportunity. Since so many different ETFs are available, the odds are great that you can find ETFs that fit your goals and investment outlook.

The Morningstar ETF website offers one of the easiest ways to view all available funds. You can also conduct a simple Internet search for "complete list of ETFs." Have fun with that!

Believe it or not, our lead portfolio manager, Josh Smith, CFA, and I would actually go through every ETF by hand each month (circa 2008 - 2012).

Up and down

The share prices of exchange-traded funds fluctuate all day as the ETF is being bought and sold. This is different from mutual funds that only trade once a day after the market closes. ETF investments can include stocks, commodities, or bonds.

ETFs are separated into categories depending on the goals and investment outlook of the fund. Here are some of the more common:

Bear market: Designed to take advantage of market downturns.

Bond: Focuses on buying and selling government and private-sector fixed income.

Commodity: Focuses on buying and selling commodities such as oil, precious metals, farm products, etc.

Currency: Focuses on buying and selling foreign currencies, companies engaged in foreign exchange, and taking advantage of changes in exchange rates. Most recently, crypto has been added to this category.

Index: Invests in stocks representing a cross-section of the stock market as a whole. For example, an Index ETF may invest in shares of companies represented in the S&P 500.

Growth and value: Focuses on stock investments in stable companies, blue-chip companies, and companies that pay moderate dividends, or on the other end of the spectrum, companies that are expected to enjoy high growth rates. Some ETFs may focus more on value stocks that can generate long-term appreciation with lower risk. Others may focus on higher-risk companies with greater potential upside.

Investment style: If you have money in a 401(k), you're probably familiar with style funds. Examples include small-capitalization funds, large-capitalization funds, lifestyle funds, etc. Some ETFs follow the same structure — for example, letting you invest in a collection of large-capitalization companies.

Industry: Focuses on investments in companies that represent specific industries, such as energy, pharmaceuticals, banking, etc.

International: Focuses on buying stocks of foreign companies or purchasing shares in index funds based on foreign exchanges.

Leveraged: Uses borrowed capital, combined with investor capital, to spread the administration and transaction costs over a larger number of investors to reduce overall fees (and hopefully increase the overall return). Tread lightly with these.

Specialty: Innovation is critical in any industry, and the investment business is no exception. In recent years, we've seen the rise of new ETFs such as tax-deferred ETFs, actively managed ETFs, and ETFs made up of other ETFs. New variations will continue to be created.

Since the list of available ETFs is so large, let's look at a few of the most popular:

If you build it ...

Kevin is co-founder of Capital Wealth Planning, LLC, in Naples, Florida. He established the firm in 2005. The firm is the sub-advisor for the Amplify CWP Enhanced Income ETF (symbol: DIVO).

Standard & Poor's 500 Index Depository Receipts: This is the first and biggest ETF. Commonly called "spider" (SPDR), it tracks the S&P 500 index, which is considered the standard for large-capitalization U.S. stock market performance. In general terms, this ETF is made up of the 500 largest publicly traded companies in the U.S.

NASDAQ 100 Index Tracking Stock: This ETF tracks the NASDAQ 100, the largest companies (based on market capitalization) listed on the NASDAQ exchange. Since the NASDAQ includes a relatively high percentage of technology companies, this ETF is a good way to invest in a diversified blend of computer, software, telecom, and biotech companies.

DIAMONDS Trust: The Dow Jones Industrial Average is made up of 30 blue-chip stocks. This ETF tracks those companies. If you want to follow the Dow, choose this ETF.

iShares S&P 500: Similar to the "spider" ETF, this fund, set up by Barclays, also tracks the S&P 500.

Standard & Poor's Mid-Cap 400: This ETF tracks the S&P Mid-Cap 400, made up of mid-size U.S. companies. If you prefer investing in medium-sized companies, this ETF might be right for you.

iShares Russell 2000: The Russell 2000 is a popular benchmark for small- to mid-cap companies, which are defined as companies with market values between $20 million and $300 million. Companies on this list tend to turn over fairly regularly as their fortunes rise and fall, but this ETF is a popular way to invest in shares of smaller companies.

iShares MSCI EAFE: This fund (Morgan Stanley Capital International and Europe, Australasia, and Far East) tracks the shares of non-U.S. companies in major world economies. If you want to invest in foreign stocks, this ETF is a convenient way.

Total Stock Market VIPERs: This ETF is set up by Vanguard Group and tracks the Wilshire 5000, which is the broadest index for U.S. stocks, and the majority of U.S. companies are included. If you want to invest in the U.S. economy as a whole, this might be the ETF for you.

Consumer Services Select Sector SPDR: Standard & Poor's has established a variety of sector ETFs. This one tracks consumer services companies.

Other services sector funds include:
- Consumer Discretionary

BACKSTORY:

The human element separates us from the rest.

There are so many quants out there — but most of the math of investing can be done by computers. It takes a person to work with clients and financial advisors, and it takes a person to help them navigate the emotions of money and their health. Aside from your health and your family, there's nothing more important than your finances. They play such a big role in your overall health and the well-being of your family.

Having emotional awareness is important, and I got that from my parents and my grandma, who I called Babcia. She had little knowledge of the stock market, but she knew about the power of saving and compounding, and she was an incredibly thoughtful, giving person.

- Energy
- Financial
- Healthcare
- Industrial
- Materials
- Technology
- Utilities

As you can see, you have a wide range of ETFs. So, what should you invest in? The answer depends on your goals and investment outlook. In general terms, if you are bullish on the U.S. economy, a fund made up of a broad cross-section of U.S. companies might be a good choice. If you think that oil stocks are poised to explode, then a sector fund focusing on oil or energy stocks could be a good choice.

It always makes sense to diversify. For example, you might choose to buy shares in a broad index fund, an international fund, and a commodities fund. That way, you have some level of protection from specific downturns in the U.S. or foreign economies, or from a rapid drop in commodities prices.

Buying covered calls: What the buyer is thinking

Understanding the buyer's perspective will help you get a good feel for the ins and outs of the process, as well as the psychology that underlies the process of writing covered calls.

The following examples are to help you see the underlying reasoning and decision-making process from the buying perspective of covered calls.

To keep the math simple, I've left out commissions of the example calculations we're about to show. I'll also use relatively round numbers just to make the math easier to follow.

Let's say today is January 1. Shares of Tech Fund XYZ are currently selling for $20 per share. Our theoretical buyer, Mr. Speculator, has been following the fund and thinks that it's poised to rise in the near future. Sales of tech stocks have been great, and Mr. Speculator thinks that new apps and advances in technology will continue to take the consumer market by storm. Instead of buying shares of Tech Fund XYZ itself, Mr. Speculator decides to purchase call options for that ETF. He buys one call option contract to purchase 100 shares of Tech Fund XYZ at $25, with a June expiration date, making it a six-month contract. The premium he pays is $3 per share, or $300.

Here's the breakdown of terms:
- Current share price: $20
- Strike price: $25
- Option premium: $3
- Expiration date: June 30
- Total cost: $300

Keep in mind the option premium price is based on factors such as the volatility of the fund (how much it tends to rise and fall), how far away the strike price is from the current price (today, about $5), and the length of the contract (six months).

Generally speaking, volatile funds and their underlying industries tend to command higher option premiums. While the strike price is 25% higher than the current price, that's not an insurmountable jump for volatile industries. On the other hand, options with a strike price of $30 will command a much lower premium amount, since that kind of rise in value requires a 50% increase in fund price in just six months.

Since the option will expire in six months, the premium is higher than an option that is expiring in 30 days. The longer the time period, the greater the chance the fund may rise in value. This also gives the buyer more time to sell the option to another investor, as well.

> **Fiscal climate**
>
> In general, covered calls tend to work best when we need them to most — during periods of higher volatility.

Option premiums will also vary greatly depending on investor outlook. If the market has declined recently and economic news is grim, option prices will be affected, just like stock prices and ETF prices. Uncertainty breeds fear, and fear goes hand-in-hand with volatility. Don't expect to see the same option prices in good times and bad times. You'll be disappointed.

While a significant amount of high-level math goes into determining option prices, in the end, the option premium is determined by what a buyer is willing to pay and what a seller is willing to accept. Time, price, and volatility are the main components of the Black-Scholes pricing model, a widely used mathematical equation used to price options contracts.

We can control two of these three inputs:

- Time: How far out do we write our calls?
- Price: What strike price do we choose?

The third component, volatility, can't be controlled. We look to harvest volatility when selling calls. They work best when we need them the most. The premiums are highest in choppy, volatile markets. They can also be counterproductive in periods of low volatility and rising markets. You need a system in place that helps you stay off a busy highway just to pick up the proverbial nickel. It's best to write calls when it makes sense to do so.

RoR

A rate of return (RoR) is the net gain or loss of an investment over a specified time period, expressed as a percentage of the investment's initial cost. When calculating the rate of return, you're determining the percentage change from the beginning of the period until the end.

Back to our example, once the option is sold, the option writer pockets the $300 option premium. It's now the seller's money.

So now what happens? If the fund price doesn't hit $25 per share, then from the call writer's point of view, nothing happens. The buyer has the right to purchase shares at $25 per share, but would only do so if that strike price plus cost ($25 + $3) is reached. In the meantime, the value of the option contract that the buyer owns fluctuates according to changes in the underlying value of Tech Fund XYZ. If the price of Tech Fund XYZ rises, the value of the option will rise, and if the fund price falls, the option value will fall.

Mr. Speculator, of course, hopes the fund price will rise. So, let's say after one month, shares of Tech Fund XYZ have gone up to $25 per share. Mr. Speculator can exercise the option and buy the shares, but he's not likely to. Why? Remember, he purchased the option contract for $3 per share. If he exercises the option contract, he pays $25 per share for the stock and if you include the $3 per share that he paid in option premiums, his total cost is $28 per share. Exercising the current contract would actually cause him to lose money, at least on paper.

Instead, he may choose to sell his option contract to another investor.

Since the share price has reached the strike price, and there are still five months left to go, the value of the option contract may now have risen to $4 or more. Mr. Speculator could sell the option contract to another investor and pocket a $1-per-share profit. While that doesn't sound like much, it's a 33% return in less than a month — not bad. In fact, that's a better rate of return than if he had purchased the stock itself — the stock has risen by 25%, but the value of the option contract increased by 33%.

In the meantime, the person who wrote the covered call simply waits to see if Mr. Speculator (or another investor if Mr. Speculator sold the contract after the first month) chooses to exercise that contract.

That's why investors buy options contracts. For this example, Mr. Speculator made a greater rate of return and tied up a lot less capital in the process.

- Buying 100 shares of Tech Fund XYZ would have cost $2,000 while he only tied up $300 buying the options.
- On the other hand, if the Tech Fund XYZ rose to $24 per share over the length of the contract, Mr. Speculator would be out $300 if he purchased options.
- If he had purchased actual shares of stock, he would be up $4 per share or $400.

> **Buying call options**
>
> To do it right, you have to accurately speculate that share values will rise to a certain level by a certain date.

Another reason speculators buy calls is that they can control a lot of notional value while putting down very little money, especially when compared to the amount required to buy actual shares. They can make big profits — and, of course, suffer big losses. Since options expire, if the shares don't move as a speculator hopes, at some point, those options are worthless, and the speculator loses their investment.

Think of it this way: If you buy call options, you have to be correct in two ways — you have to accurately speculate that share values will rise to a certain level, and you have to guess it will do by a certain date. Not so easy.

Intrinsic value and time value

The value of an option contract is based on two main factors: intrinsic value and the value of time. Let's look at both.

Intrinsic value is what an asset is worth in and of itself. For example, if you buy shares of an ETF, those shares have an intrinsic value — the amount you, or another person, are willing to pay to own those shares. If you purchase 100 shares of Tech Fund XYZ for $20 per share, the intrinsic value of those 100 shares is $2,000.

In options terms, an option contract has an intrinsic value when the share price is above the strike price for that contract. Why? The contract can be exercised and shares can be purchased for the strike price. In effect, the intrinsic value is the difference between the strike price and the current market price — if the market price is $21 and the strike price is $20, an option contract for a single share has an intrinsic value of $1.

Time value is what an option contract is worth based on the amount of time before it expires. An easy way to calculate time value is to subtract the intrinsic value of an option from the premium price. For example, if an option contract has a strike price of $20, the market price is $21, and the contract still has four months left before it expires, the option premium may be $2 (or more). In that case, the time value is $1 ($2 option premium minus $1 intrinsic value).

What if the option is currently out-of-the-money? The entire premium is based on time value since there is no intrinsic value. Here's a simple way to differentiate the two: Intrinsic value is the amount the option is in-the-money. Time value is the additional amount of the option premium.

In our recommended strategy, you'll sell covered calls at out-of-the-money strike prices. That way you can hold on to the underlying shares, enjoy dividends, pocket the option premiums as additional income, and gain from appreciation in the underlying value of the shares up to the strike price. In those cases, buyers pay you for the time value of the option and there is no intrinsic value.

Back to the buyer

When we last saw Mr. Speculator, he was pleased that shares of Tech Fund XYZ rose to the strike price. But what happens if the fund shares don't hit the strike price? For one thing, no one will be surprised. That's because roughly 70% of options contracts that started as out-of-the-money contracts expire as out-of-the-money contracts. ETFs, like stocks, don't tend to appreciate rapidly across the board, especially over the short term.

Thus, Mr. Speculator has choices as time passes. If he starts to doubt his investment, he could sell the contract to another investor. Let's say he waits three months ... because the time until expiration is now shorter, the time value of the contract is likely to be lower, possibly more than half. He may be able to sell the contract for $1 or $1.50 per share, and while he loses money, at least he won't lose his entire investment. He could also decide to hang on. But the longer he waits, the less time value the option contract has, and the less it will be worth.

Of course, the stock could rise to $23 or $24 a share. In that case, the value of the option is likely to increase, since the chances of the stock hitting the strike price have become much greater.

What's the bottom line?

The value of an option contract is a complicated dance between the value of the underlying shares and the time remaining before the contract expires. Since the option will eventually expire, buying options is a risky proposition, which is why many times it's more advantageous to be on the selling side of options investing. That's what you are doing when you write covered calls.

Let's take a closer look.

Writing covered calls: What you're thinking

Let's pretend that on January 1 you bought 100 shares of Tech Fund XYZ for $20. You're delighted and surprised to find a tech fund that pays a dividend.

Alas, the power of the pen and the textbook. The fund pays a dividend of 2%, but you want to increase your rate of return, so you decide to write covered calls on those shares.

First, you give the matter some thought. You're bullish on the technology sector, but you don't think those stocks will rise significantly in the near future — you know tech companies are making handsome profits, but you feel those considerations are already built into the value of their stocks. So, you think it's unlikely the price of shares of Tech Fund XYZ will go up more than 25%.

Let's look at the possibilities open to you:

Strike Price   Expiration Dates and Option Prices

Strike Price	Feb.	April	June
$20	$0.50	$1.40	$4.00
$25	$0.10	$0.30	$3.00
$30	$0.04	$0.12	$0.30

This chart is hypothetical to make it easier to identify a good opportunity. With practice, you'll spot the right strike price and expiration date for your situation and goals.

Remember, it's January, and you check the different option prices and are drawn to the return you could get from selling a six-month call at $25 a share. Three dollars per share in option premium is an outstanding return. After all, that's a 15% return in just six months from the premium alone.

You're more than happy to make that deal, so you write a covered call under those terms. Within a day or so the $300 hits your account. You can spend it, invest it, park in a money market fund for the time being, or do whatever you want to do. It's your money to spend — whether the underlying position ultimately goes up, down, or sideways.

In review, what has happened so far? You spent $2,000 on shares of Tech Fund XYZ. You'll receive a 2% dividend (on an annual basis) on those shares. You also received $300, or a 15% return, from writing the covered call expiring in six months.

Now you simply wait and watch for the following share reactions and outcomes:

- **Stay flat:** You're a little disappointed, but you're still the proud recipient of the option premiums you sold.
- **Fall by $2 a share to $18:** You're more disappointed, but you still haven't lost money. The option premium covered the loss in underlying value of shares. By writing covered calls you've hedged your investment, to some extent.
- **Increase by $2 a share to $22:** You're happier — not only have you already made a 15% return, but the underlying value of your shares has increased by 10%.
- **Rise to $25 per share, and the contract is exercised on the expiration date:** You're a teeny bit disappointed to see shares

in such a great-performing asset go, but you console yourself with the fact you sold those shares for a 25% profit. Plus, you received dividend payments and you made 15% writing covered calls. In the end, you're really not that disappointed, are you? You take your proceeds, buy shares in another name, then rinse and repeat. Of course, if the underlying asset skyrockets to $30 or higher, you may be annoyed that you left some upside capture on the table. It happens from time to time when you write covered calls. But keep in mind what someone much smarter than I would say: "You never lose money taking a profit."

As we discussed, most options contracts expire out-of-the money. If that happens, and you still want to hold on to shares of Tech Fund XYZ, you'll repeat the process. Remember, option premiums will have changed, possibly dramatically, depending on the underlying value of the shares and the volatility of the broader markets.

For example, if the share price has risen to $24, a six-month contract with a strike price of $25 could be worth more than $3 per share. If you want to increase your chances for holding on to those shares, you may choose to write a covered call with a strike price of $30 per share — you'll receive less in option premiums, but this lowers the chances that option will be exercised.

Here's an easy way to choose which option contract terms are right for you. Ask yourself these questions:

Do I think shares will rise dramatically in value over the short term?

If yes, do the following:

Don't write covered calls at first. Give it the chance to increase in value without any risk of an option being exercised.

Write out-of-the-money calls. For example, if the current price is $20 per share and you think $28 is a likely near-term target price, write covered calls at $30 per share. You'll receive less in option premiums, but you'll enjoy a greater upside if the fund increases rapidly in value as you expected.

Do I think the shares might fall in value in the near future? If yes, do the following:

Consider selling those shares and investing in something you feel has better prospects. Ask yourself why you would own what you think will decrease in value.

Write in-the-money calls. The premium price will be higher and will help to offset short-term losses in share price. Of course, if you're wrong and the fund increases in value, it's likely the option will be exercised, and you'll lose those shares.

Do I think the price will stay flat or only increase slightly in value? If yes, do the following:

Maximize your return by writing calls with strike prices relatively close to the current market price. That way, you'll maximize the option premium you receive, and as a result you'll maximize your rate of return. Even if the market stays flat, you'll do better than the average investor while slightly reducing your risk profile.

Consider writing calls with short-term expiration dates. If the economic climate changes, you won't be locked into long-term calls at lower than current market value premiums.

It's worth reiterating that no investment system is completely risk-free. If the market tanks and your shares decline in value, you may lose money, despite the fact that you received option premiums on the calls you sold.

But if you've written covered calls, you'll always lose less money than if you had not written covered calls — the option premium will help offset some of your losses.

A covered call is not just "covered" because you own the underlying asset, writing a covered call also offers you some amount of "cover" from falling share prices.

Writing covered calls: Digging deeper into the process

The examples we just worked through were fairly straightforward. Now, let's use a real-world example to help you determine the right covered call option terms for your situation.

We'll use the SPDR S&P 500 ETF Trust. If you're scoring at home, the ticker symbol for this ETF is SPY. We'll use that symbol to refer to this ETF from now on. You chose the SPDR S&P 500 ETF Trust because it "seeks investment results that correspond generally to the price and yield performance, before fees and expenses, of U.S. large-cap stocks, as represented by the Standard & Poor's 500 Index."

As I sit here writing this, the SPY share price is $445. However, by the time you read this the share price, option prices, etc., are certain to be different, so this example should be used for informational purposes only.

As always, you're hoping the U.S. economy is headed up, and you want to profit from that. So, you buy 100 shares of SPY for $44,562.20. To make the math simpler, we're leaving commissions out of this example.

Tracking prices

Here are option prices, and we'll pretend this in mid-October, so the first expiration date is a month away.

Note: The first draft of this book was written a while back. At the time, SPY was trading at $105.45. Yes, I've been working on this book for a while. Hey, I have a day job.

Strike Price	Expiration Date
	November
$435.00	$15.20
$440.00	$11.10
$445.00	$7.00
$450.00	$4.50
$455.00	$2.50

Strike Price	Expiration Date
	December
$460.00	$3.60
$465.00	$2.30
$470.00	$1.44
$475.00	$0.89

Strike Price	Expiration Date
	March
$440.00	$22.60
$445.00	$19.30
$450.00	$16.20
$460.00	$10.87

What should you do? First let's do some math. Using the same information from the example above, we'll assume you paid $445 for your shares, and we'll apply simple calculations.

Figuring out your strategy

First, we'll determine the value of the option. For example, the premium for a November strike price of $435 is $15.20. While you'll receive $15.20 per share, the strike price is $10 below what you paid for it. If the option is exercised, you'll receive $10 less than you paid per share and, as a result, the option is worth only $5.20 in total to you ($15.20 - $10 = $5.20). The value is $5.20.

Next, we'll determine your rate of return. To keep things simple, we'll just apply the value to your purchase price. As an example, $5.20 divided by $445 is 0.0116. That rate is for about a month, so we'll annualize that rate (in this case, multiply it by 12) to calculate an annual rate of return. That way you'll always compare apples to apples. So, 0.0116 times 12 is 14%. In that instance your annual rate is 14%.

Expiration Date: November

Strike Price	Premium	Value	Rate of Return	Annual Rate
$435.00	$15.20	$5.20	1.16%	14.02%
$440.00	$11.10	$6.10	1.37%	16.44%
$445.00	$7.00	$7.00	1.57%	18.87%
$450.00	$4.50	$4.50	1.01%	12.13%
$455.00	$2.50	$2.50	0.55%	6.50%

Expiration Date: December

Strike Price	Premium	Value	Rate of Return	Annual Rate
$460.00	$3.20	$3.60	0.81%	4.80%
$465.00	$2.15	$2.30	0.51%	3.10%
$470.00	$1.80	$1.44	0.32%	1.90%
$475.00	$0.95	$0.89	0.20%	1.20%

Expiration Date: March

Strike Price	Premium	Value	Rate of Return	Annual Rate
$440.00	$22.60	$17.60	3.95%	9.49%
$445.00	$19.30	$19.30	4.33%	10.41%
$455.00	$16.20	$16.20	3.64%	8.70%
$465.00	$10.87	$10.80	2.42%	5.82%

Sometimes these numbers will look too good to be true. In fact, they often are. While those are the last premium prices those options traded at in the last 24 hours, occasionally no buyers or sellers stepped up to complete transactions at those prices. So, you may be looking at a stale quote. Make sure you keep tabs on the recent volume, as well, to see how many options have traded — that will give you a good indication of whether you can find a buyer willing to make a trade at the price you're expecting.

By the way, that's also a great reason to include limits in your options trades — if you just place a "market" order, you may find yourself writing a covered call at a dramatically lower price than you expected.

Now, let's look at the December category. The $460 strike price option generates a pretty nice annual return rate — that one might be worth exploring. At $460, the contract may very well be exercised. But if you get the return you want, that's one situation where taking part in an execution is fine by you.

But what if there are no buyers at that rate? That's OK. What about the $465 strike price? The annual rate of return is over 3%. Combine that with the 1.27% dividend yield and your annual return is over 4%. Plus, if SPY does hit $465 per share and the contract is exercised, you'll make a profit of $20 per share, or $2,000.

Here's the result if those things occur:

- Option premium: $230
- Dividend: $94 (SPY pays quarterly, so we won't count this two-month accrued dividend in our calculation.)
- Share value profit: $2,000
- Total profit: $2,230
- Rate of return 5.01% (in two months!)

For that kind of return, do you mind if the option is exercised? The answer is no. Now, there's no guarantee that the S&P 500 will advance 2.2% to put the shares in-the-money. But, it's not an unrealistic reach.

What should you do?

When considering your strategy for moving forward with options, first, do basic math (just like I showed you in the previous example). Then step back and consider the possibilities.

The key is to analyze rates of return, your investment goals, and your

BACKSTORY:

One of the people who influenced me most was a bad guy.

Let me explain. This broker wasn't a good person, and he certainly didn't care about his clients. He tried to take advantage of people over the phone and bullied them into buying things. One time in particular, he convinced a client to put in a buy order for a penny stock that earned the salesman a high commission. After which, the client had to send in a check to pay for the trade — if he didn't, the broker would be responsible for the trade and it would be called a "DK," as in, I "don't know" where the money is. In that situation, the firm doesn't eat the loss, the broker does.

Turns out, the stock that the broker bullied the client into purchasing was a bad decision. For three days straight, we could hear the broker on the phone, several times a day, calling the client trying to get the check. While most of us in the office were very young, we weren't naïve to the world, and we were sure the client wasn't going to send in the check. The broker should've closed out the position, taken a small loss, and moved on. But his ego got the best of him, and he continued this argument for several days straight.

At the end of the week, an envelope arrived from the client. The broker was strutting around the office like a peacock, holding up the envelope, saying, "I told ya I'd get it. I told ya I'd get it." And right in front of everybody, he opens the envelope and pulls out

a piece of paper. On that piece of paper was a big red Sharpie checkmark that said, "Your check."

The loss was taken out of the broker's paycheck, and shortly thereafter, he left. He wasn't cut out for this business, he wasn't good at picking stocks, wasn't good with people, and he treated the trainees even worse. He'd make us come in at night and do cold calls, standing over us, berating us, and chewing with his mouth open while we tried to execute trades.

For me, this guy was an incredible lesson in what not to do. Sometimes you need to see things done the wrong way so you know the right way to do it.

short- and long-term outlook for the underlying position. As I mentioned earlier, if you think SPY is likely to rise dramatically in value, you might be better off choosing a higher strike price and a shorter expiration date. In this example, a nice balance between the two could be the December $470 option with a premium of $1.44 — you'll enjoy a roughly 2% rate of return, you'll potentially receive dividend payouts, and the shares can increase by almost $25 per share before the options could be exercised. If they rise by $20 per share by the expiration date, you'll have made a paper profit of $2,000, plus an additional return of over $144 in option premiums. Then take a breath, do it again, and attempt to make more money.

Now, let's look at the opposite case. Say you feel SPY could tread water for the next six months. You hope not, but it's possible based on current market conditions. Increase your return by writing a covered call with a strike price closer to the current price — but with a longer expiration date.

A good choice could be the March $455 strike price. If the shares stay flat, that's OK, because you'll receive an option premium with a nearly 9% annualized return, plus you'll receive dividends ... and if the fund rises above $455 per share, you'll make a profit on the underlying shares, as well.

Since you don't think the shares will perform well in the next six months, you feel there's little risk the stock will jump dramatically in value — say, to $500 per share, and there's little risk that your contract will be exercised before you enjoy all those profits. If exercised, you still made a nice return on your covered calls while slightly hedging your downside.

General strategy guidelines

I hope that you feel better about the process after following these examples. Now, let's step back and look at basic guidelines you can apply to writing covered calls. My goal is to help you understand what to do in your specific situation.

Remember, your goal is to follow a strategy that lets you reach your investment objectives, so let's cover some of the basics of making that happen.

Guideline 1: What expiration dates mean to you

Your goal could be to maximize the rate of return on the covered calls you write, but at times you may want to accept a lower rate of return so you can take advantage of appreciation possibilities and total return. As I mentioned, sometimes it makes sense to write a covered call for a lower price if doing so gives you room to enjoy a rise in the stock price.

It's important to maximize your overall return — not just your covered call return. Expiration dates are key to making that happen.

As a rule of thumb, the shorter the expiration date, the lower the price of the option. If an option will expire in a week, that's not a lot of time for the stock to rise in value, so option buyers won't be willing to pay a lot to own that option. That's not necessarily bad for you — if you feel the shares are likely to rise significantly in the next few months, you may be willing to take a small return now while you hold the position and enjoy a greater return later.

Remember, every situation isn't ideal for covered call writing. Sometimes it's better to leave a position uncovered when the juice isn't worth the squeeze. Always do the math.

If you think that might be the case, write short-term covered calls at strike prices several dollars higher than the current market price or do nothing at all. For example, if you own a stock with a market price of $36 per share, and you write a covered call with a strike price of $40 per share, expiring in a month, the chances are slim the shares will jump to $40 a share over a very short timeframe.

That's why most options increase in price as the expiration date gets farther out — investors are willing to pay more for a contract that expires at a relatively distant time in the future. And the reverse is true: Investors will pay less for an option that expires soon than they will for an option that expires down the road.

The differences in premium amounts tend to flatten out. For example, the difference between the premium for an option expiring in a month and an option expiring in six months is much greater than the difference between options expiring in four months and six months.

Here's a quick example

Strike Price	1 month	2 months	4 months	6 months
$100	$0.85	$2.20	$3.40	$3.80

The difference in return slows down between the four-month and six-month options ... and it speeds up between the one-month and two-month options. As the expiration date gets closer, the option is worth a lot less because the likelihood it will expire out-of-the-money increases dramatically. In technical terms, this is known as theta decay. On the other end of the scale, investors typically assume that if a stock has stayed relatively flat for four months, it may not remain relatively flat for six months ... they'll pay a little more for a longer expiration date.

Let's take a look at differences in writing short-term and long-term covered calls:

Short-term covered calls:

- Have a lower possibility it may be exercised, especially if you write the call at an out-of-the-money price.

- Can provide a higher total investment yield (depending on volatility).

- Make it possible to enjoy higher appreciation over time, since the likelihood of the option being exercised is lower and you can adjust your strike price higher each time you repeat the process, giving you a better chance of holding on to the underlying shares.

- Require increased execution or brokerage transactions, fees, and commissions over time. However, this is much less of an issue than it used to be.

Long-term covered calls:

- Generate a higher total premium and produce immediate income, since that income is placed in your account almost immediately.

- Require fewer brokerage transactions and commissions, since you will write fewer covered calls over the course of a year. Again, not as big of a deal these days.

- Provide greater downside protection in case the value of the underlying shares decreases. After all, the higher the option premium, the more "covered" you are in the case of a market downturn.

- Can offer tax advantages due to subsequent-year expiration dates, or if you use long-dated options (LEAPS).

What should you do?

In my opinion, diversification applies not just to stock selection but also to expiration dates. If you own shares in four different companies, write covered calls creating a balance of shorter-term and longer-term expiration dates. That way you'll enjoy larger premiums in some cases while keeping your options open (pun intended) by writing covered calls with shorter expiration dates in other cases.

If the market dips, you'll have a little more protection because you wrote calls with higher premiums. If the market explodes, you should be able to hang on to some of your positions, enjoy the capital appreciation, and continue to write covered calls at higher strike prices so you can maximize your capital returns and your option premiums.

The same logic applies if you own hundreds of shares in one company. Feel free to write covered calls on a portion of the shares with short-term expiration dates, and write covered calls on the remaining shares with longer-term expiration dates. You'll spread your risk, maintain flexibility, and no matter which way the market goes you'll be able to take advantage.

Guideline 2: What strike prices mean to you

Now let's look at general guidelines where strike prices are concerned.

Here's a sample chart for a stock trading at $102, with an expiration date about six months out:

Strike Price	Option Premium	Return Rate
$102.50	$6.10	5.90%
$105.00	$4.20	4.10%
$107.50	$2.95	2.80%

The best return rate is generated from writing a covered call for an option with the $102.50 strike price.

That makes sense, since the stock will only have to increase in value by $0.50 before the option is in-the-money.

But let's take it a step further. What happens if the underlying shares increase in value and the option is exercised at each strike price? Here's the result:

Strike Price	Total Return	Return Rate
$102.50	$0.50	0.40%
$105	$3	2.90%
$107.50	$5.50	5.30%

Let's add the option premium to the appreciation and calculate the total return (without taking dividends into account):

Strike Price	Appreciation	Return Rate
$102.50	$6.50	6.30%
$105	$7.20	7.00%
$107.50	$8.45	8.20%

RoR 2.0

Pay attention to expiration dates and strike prices, but pay the most attention to your rate of return — that's what will help you build and maintain your wealth over the long term.

The return rates are shown on a six-month, not annual, basis. To calculate an annual rate of return, simply double the return rate shown.

What did you learn? Hopefully, something you already understand: Your total return is based not just on the premium you receive from writing covered calls, but also on capital gains from a rise in stock prices (and from receiving dividends from those funds). Balancing the strike price with the expiration date gives you the best chance of maximizing your return while maintaining flexibility.

You also should recognize the return rate column. In these hypothetical examples, they're based on the stock hitting the strike price and the options being exercised — and, therefore, you receive the strike price in return for selling your shares.

If the stock doesn't hit the strike price, you keep the option premium, but you won't realize any capital gain from selling the shares themselves. So, in basic terms, the rate of the option premium should play heavily into your decision-making process — and that rate is heavily influenced by the expiration date.

Think of it this way: If you write a covered call at a strike price of $55, expiring in six months, for 100 shares of an stock trading at $50, and you receive $2.50 per share in option premiums, then the $250 you receive is a guaranteed return and comes in at an annual rate of 10% before commissions and fees. If the stock rises in value and the option is exercised, so much the better, but your option premium provides a "floor" return.

I'll say it again, every investment carries risk. Even putting money in a savings account carries an amount of risk, however small it is. Ask people whose deposits exceeded FDIC limits about what happened when their banks failed.

That's why it's worth repeating: The key to building wealth is to maximize return while minimizing risk. We can't eliminate risk, but we can be creative enough to minimize it.

For new investors, buying ETF shares is a great way to diversify your investments and reduce the chances of incurring single specific stock risk. Writing covered calls is a great way to further minimize risk and achieve additional returns in bullish or bearish market conditions, year after year, while you watch your wealth grow.

Remember the table I showed you in the preface? If you invest $100,000 in a 401(k) and get a 5% return, after 30 years you'll have roughly $430,000. If you invest the same $100,000 and get a 10% return, you'll have over $1.7 million in your account.

That's a huge difference.

I've always felt the pain of discipline is far less than the pain of regret.

Writing covered calls on dividend stocks

Writing or selling covered calls is a conservative way to earn extra income on top of the dividend income you already receive on dividend-paying stocks you own. You can sell one contract for every 100 shares you own and collect an option premium in return.

When selling covered calls involving dividend-paying stocks, you hope to keep the shares in order to continue collecting dividends plus the potential for appreciation.

If the stock price remains below the option's strike price until the expiration date, the option expires and you retain your shares. You can repeat the exercise and generate more option income, and as long as you retain your shares, you'll continue to collect dividends.

On the other hand, if the stock price moves above the strike price, the option holder will likely exercise the option and call away your shares. In that case, you'll be paid the option's strike price per share. Since you no longer own the shares, you'll forgo future dividend payments until you reinvest the proceeds.

Why use dividend stocks

Deciding which stocks are attractive option-writing candidates is an important tactic. Since one of the main sources of return is the dividend, stocks selected for covered call writing should have generous and secure dividend yields. Ideally, the yield will exceed the yields on both the S&P 500 index and 10-year treasury notes. The dividend yield provides a significant part of the desired return. Keep in mind, we're not looking for the highest dividends. Lean toward companies that are increasing your dividends at a regular clip.

If it's sustainable, the dividends will also tend to support the stock price even when the overall market is under pressure. If the company has a strong position within its served market and earns a profit rate that comfortably covers the dividend, then a generous dividend rate offers enough protection to hedge against some losses in a declining market. So, you can get paid while you wait for better times.

The company would also ideally offer growth potential in addition to its attractive and sustainable dividend yield.

As a covered call option writer, you would aim to capture some of this price appreciation potential by writing calls that are a bit out-of-the-money, where the strike price is above the current stock price. You can gain insight into the company's growth potential by looking at analysts' forecasts and the recent earnings and dividend history.

Stocks with generous and sustainable dividends that are expected to grow are typically attractive candidates for a covered-call portfolio. Two lists of potentially attractive stocks for covered writing are the 30 stocks making up the Dow Jones industrial average and the stocks in the S&P 500 Dividend Aristocrats index mentioned in Chapter 4.

Stocks selected for the Dow tend to be mature industry leaders that pay generous dividends in many cases. As we mentioned, Dividend Aristocrats are stocks that have increased their dividends annually for at least the last

25 years. These stocks also have sustainable dividends, based on their past performance. Dividend Aristocrats with high yields are reasonable candidates for covered call writing. I like the Aristocrats, but 25 years is a long time. I prefer companies with a 10 - 15% dividend growth average for the past five years.

Pricing and timing

Once you've identified attractive candidates for covered call writing, it's time to examine the stock's option pricing. Some of the factors that make a stock attractive for writing a covered call may also reduce the option price. Stocks with a modest degree of anticipated volatility and high dividend yields tend to have lower call premiums than more volatile stocks with little or no dividend yield. Since the goal is to produce consistently attractive returns, choosing stocks that are less volatile with decent dividend yields is often a good compromise.

Options can be written at various strike prices and with various expiration dates.

To capture upside from the stock's potential price appreciation, you should write the option out-of-the-money (strike price above the current stock price). The further the option is out-of-the-money, the greater the potential upside from price appreciation, but the lower the market price of the option.

Dogs of the Dow

The 10 Dow stocks with the highest yields are called the Dogs of the Dow, most of which would be classified as value stocks. I tend to stay away from these names as a group. They're often "dogs" for a reason. But don't ignore it when you're looking for individual opportunities. Not all of the dogs have fleas.

For example, nine-month CSX calls with strikes of $36, $37, and $38 were selling for $1.33, $0.83, and $0.57, respectively. The more optimistic you are about the stock's potential price appreciation, the further out-of-the-money the option can be written. Selecting a higher strike price option could result in a significantly greater upside. In the CSX example, writing calls with a strike of $38 rather than $37 would mean receiving $0.26 less ($0.83 - $0.57) for writing the option. The potential gain from price appreciation would, however, rise by $1 ($38

BACKSTORY:

I think he almost had a heart attack when I told him I manage more than a billion dollars.

My first day on the job, my mentor, Bill Bierlin, came to my desk and told me everything I thought I knew about investing and money management was wrong. Bill was a taskmaster with a heart of gold. I was very lucky to learn so much from him.

The best lesson he ever gave me wasn't to keep my hair cut. One morning when I first started the job, I was at the desk and heard movement behind me. I saw a hand drop a $10 bill on my desk. I turned and saw Bill looking at me as he was walking away. I held up the $10 bill and said, "What's this?" He made a clipping gesture with his fingers to his hair. I quickly realized he was telling me to get a haircut (for the record, I had just gotten a haircut the day before). I had to leave the office and go get another trim. That would happen frequently.

It wasn't to wear button-down collared shirts (I wore them for so many years that you'll rarely see me in one). One Friday, the office was preparing for a golf event. I'm no golfer, but I was still new and happy to participate. I came into the office wearing a nice golf shirt and pants. I sat at my desk and felt a tap on my shoulder. Of course, Bill was standing there. As I'm going through my mental checklist, "I don't think my hair is that long ... I have a collared shirt on ..." he said, "You have a short-sleeved shirt on. Do you have a short-sleeved jacket to go with it?" I said, "No, I have a golf shirt on, we're taking the client to the golf event." Bill replied, "We're not at the golf event, we're at the office." I promptly got up, went home, and came back with a suit on.

Bill Bierlin

The best lesson was about stop-loss orders. Bill was completely opposed to them. Under no circumstances were we going to be lazy and put in a stop-loss order. Stop-loss orders are a very common practice for investors. Simply, if a stock drops to a certain point, you must execute the sell to get the investor out. It's a theory that allows you to keep your losses small and not have to monitor the trade all the time. When Bill explained his theory, it was 1994, a time before we had computer-based order entry. We had specialists on the floor of the Exchange, and you'd tell one of them to put in that sell order. During the day, they'd bring it down, take that sell order below the sell point, execute that stop order, and the investor will be out of that position. However, usually by the end of the day the stock would be back up again. So, Bill told me not to put in stop-loss orders for that reason. And I still don't.

Bill and I stayed in touch over the years and, in the summer of 2019, we had lunch near his home outside Philadelphia. That time together allowed me to thank him for all he did for me. I think he almost had a heart attack that day when I told him that I manage more than a billion dollars. Now, as I'm writing this in 2021, we manage more than $5 billion — I wish he were alive to hear that.

- $37), thereby increasing the potential upside by $0.74 ($1 - $0.26). This greater upside may seem attractive, but if the stock price falls or doesn't rise much, the lower strike option would have produced a better outcome.

The call writer must also decide how long an option to write. In the CSX example, options were listed with expirations of one, two, three, six, nine, and 21 months away. As the length of the option's term increases, its price increases, but generally at a decreasing rate. For the CSX options with a strike of $37 and terms of one, two, three, six, nine, and 21 months, the prices were $0.05, $0.12, $0.22, $0.43, $0.59, $0.83 and $1.57. While the market price increases as the term is lengthened, the rate per month usually declines as length rises. Thus, the option writer might be able to earn a somewhat higher return per period by writing shorter-term options. Such an approach has significant disadvantages, however. Specifically, the more times you must buy and sell options and stock, the greater the transaction costs and the greater the likelihood of adverse tax results.

Hence, under certain conditions, you may want to set up your initial covered call positions with longer options.

Key calculations

Before actually assembling a covered position, you should make several calculations.

First, figure out the return if the stock is at the same price at the option's expiration as it was when purchased. In this case, the gain would be equal to the sum of the dividends to be received plus the proceeds from the option sale. The return would be this gain divided by the cost of the position. For example, if the stock had a 3.5% dividend yield and the call was sold for a price equal to 4% of the stock's price, the position would produce a total return of about 7.5%. An attractive covered position should generate a decent return in this circumstance. In the CSX example, this was approximately 6.2%.

Second, calculate how far the stock's price would have to fall before the position would show a loss. This is the same percentage as the gain on the transaction if the stock price didn't change — the sum of the dividends and proceeds from the option sale. Remember, if the stock falls further, the position will show a loss. In the CSX example, the stock would have to fall by $2.29 to $34.71 (a decline of about 6.2%) before the position would show a loss (assuming the expected dividends are paid). The price of $33.39 represents the breakeven point. As long as the stock's price stays above this level, the position will show a profit.

Third, figure out the maximum gain on the position. This is the sum of the dividends and option proceeds plus the difference between the option's strike price and the cost of the stock. For a nine-month call, the annual return is this sum divided by the cost of the position, which has already been calculated above. In the CSX example, the maximum gain on the position would be 10.1% (14% annualized). In more aggressive call writing using options with a strike of $38, the potential gain would be 14.0% (18.7% annualized).

The covered option position should only be established if the investor finds each of these calculated numbers attractive.

Receiving your dividends

Now, your hard work pays off! You receive the dividend on the day the company establishes the record date. Those who own the stock on that date will be paid the dividend even if they sell their shares before the checks are sent out. Because settlement of trades takes three business days, you must have purchased the stock three or more days prior to the record date to receive the dividend. The first day after the last day for owning the stock and being paid the dividend is called the ex-dividend date. The stock's price will typically fall on its ex-dividend date by about the amount of the dividend. In the case of CSX, with a dividend of $0.09 per quarter, the stock price will tend to open about $0.09 lower on the ex-dividend date than the price at which it closed the day before. When you trade options, keep an eye on ex-dividend dates of stocks with written options.

Fundamental strengths

Promising dividend stocks can be identified by looking at markers of fiscal strength, such as predictable cash flows, good value plus performance, company stability, and dividend metrics.

Outcomes

In a portfolio approach to covered call writing, your goal is to have a steady, attractive return. When the market is rising rapidly, returns from

Which of these situations makes you feel more comfortable?
As you read on, the difference will become clear how each can affect your bottom line over the long term.

- You own stocks in a company that might pay you a smaller dividend today but is enjoying higher sales and profits each passing year.

- You own stocks in a company that pays you a large dividend today and is seeing a slow and steady return.

a covered call strategy may lag behind the market and leave some unrealized upside profits on the table. However, a covered call strategy shines in a range-bound (where the price bounces between specific high and low prices), declining, or volatile market, where the income generated by option writing along with reliable dividend-paying stocks selected for the portfolio modestly hedges against some of the potential downside in the market, and helps the portfolio's return be significantly higher than the market average on a risk-adjusted basis.

In addition to factors I previously mentioned in assessing the fundamentals of a company, you can identify a promising dividend stock by its historical dividend payments. See if they are rising over time. Look for fiscal strength of the company: predictable cash flows, good value, consistent performance, and stability of the company through a financial snapshot from its balance sheet, cash flow, and profit/loss statements.

In the United States, boards of directors won't raise the dividend if they believe they will have to stop, turn around, and cut it. Thus, an increasing dividend rate on a per-share basis indicates a vote of confidence from people at the company with the closest, real-time access to the company's latest financial reports. It's not perfect, errors happen, and financial deception from company executives occurs, but the board's actions to raise the dividend can be taken as a positive indicator of the company's success.

Dividends can offer significant returns. For example, the Dividend Aristocrats have generated solid annualized total returns over the last decade. The Dividend Aristocrats, as we highlighted previously, did so with less volatility over the last decade.

So, how do you identify a promising dividend stock? Dividend investing requires an understanding of company fundamentals like any other investment with specific emphasis on dividend metrics.

Using high-dividend stocks

Dividend yield is one of the main factors to consider when investing in dividend-paying stocks. You need to be wary of too high a dividend yield, say 5% or above because they're usually more risky investments. As of June 2021, Warren Buffett's company, Berkshire Hathaway, owns 48 stocks, according to a recent 13F filing with the U.S. Securities and Exchange Commission (SEC). These holdings are filled with top dividend plays that can be used by income investors to generate passive earnings and consistent dividend growth.

Top 10 Berkshire Hathaway stocks
(as of August 2018)

Ticker	Company	Annualized Dividend	Closing Price	Dividend Yield Payout	Berkshire's Ownership ($ million)
STOR	Store Capital	$1.24	$25.83	4.80%	$462.19
SNY	Sanofi	$1.86	$38.93	4.78%	$148.34
KHC	Kraft-Heinz	$2.50	$56.58	4.42%	$20,283.79
GM	General Motors	$1.52	$38.28	3.97%	$1,816.99
KO	Coca-Cola	$1.56	$42.25	3.69%	$17,371.99
QSR	Restaurant Brands International	$1.80	$56.95	3.16%	$480.30
WFC	Wells Fargo	$1.56	$55.26	2.82%	$23,925.86
PSX	Phillips 66	$3.20	$118.75	2.69%	$4,382.58
WMT	Wal-Mart Stores	$2.08	$83.37	2.49%	$123.98
USB	U.S. Bancorp	$1.20	$51.06	2.35%	$4,587.81

Yield versus growth

There are two popular schools of thought regarding dividend investing: yield and growth. Each has its merits and drawbacks.

Yield puts more emphasis on stocks that are high-yielding today, rather than on how much they can grow. The growth approach emphasizes companies with the ability to develop payouts over time, even if the yield isn't that attractive when compared to other stocks.

Some of the most important metrics used to determine a dividend's strength include price-to-earnings ratio, dividend payout ratio, and debt-to-equity ratio. They are essential aspects in analyzing a company's fundamentals and evaluating its financial strength and growth potential.

Focus on company fundamentals

Fundamental analysis is the process of looking at a business at the most basic or fundamental financial level. This type of analysis examines the key ratios of a business to determine its financial health. It also can give you an idea of the value of its stock. It takes several factors into account, including revenue, asset management, and interest rate. Investors often focus on the earnings of the company because this indicates the health and profitability of the company.

In addition to studying a company's earnings, you'll need fundamental analysis tools that focus on earnings, growth, and value in the market. These are some of the essentials:

Earnings per share (EPS): This tells you how much of a company's profit is assigned to each share of stock. Earnings per share is calculated as net income, minus dividends on preferred stock, divided by the number of outstanding shares.

Price-to-earnings ratio (P/E): This compares the current sales price of a company's stock to its per-share earnings. Seen as the most-used valuation metric, P/E ratios are typically used for evaluating mature companies, so it's important for comparing dividend stocks.

Projected earnings growth (PEG): This anticipates the one-year-earnings growth rate of the stock.

Price-to-sales ratio (P/S): This values a company's stock price compared to its revenues. It's sometimes called the PSR, revenue multiple, or sales multiple.

Price-to-book ratio (P/B): This ratio, also known as the price-to-equity ratio, compares a stock's book value to its market value. You arrive at it by dividing the stock's most recent closing price by last quarter's book value per share. Book value is the value of an asset as it appears in the company's books. It's equal to the cost of each asset less cumulative depreciation.

Dividend payout ratio: This compares dividends paid to stockholders to the company's total net income. It accounts for retained earnings — income that isn't paid out but rather retained for potential growth. As mentioned in Chapter 4 on the basics of dividend investing, payout ratio is the stock's dividend as a percentage of its earnings and shows a stock's ability to continue to pay its dividend, even if profits decline temporarily.

Dividend yield: This, too, is a ratio: Yearly dividends compared to share price. It's expressed as a percentage. Divide dividends paid in a one-year period per share by the value of a share.

Return on equity: Divide the company's net income by shareholders' equity to find the return on equity. You might also hear this expressed as the company's return on net worth.

Total return: The combination of dividends and share-price appreciation. This is the overall picture of a dividend stock's performance. If a stock rises by 6% this year and pays a 3% dividend yield, its total return is 9%.

EPS growth: Reflects the stock's continued growth. Consistently growing earnings are a good indicator that a stock will continue to grow its dividend.

If you don't intend to use dividends for immediate income and are investing for the long run, you can reinvest your dividends. This will help you maximize your total return through old-fashioned dollar-cost-averaging and the power of compounding.

You can do this via a dividend reinvestment plan (DRIP) that automatically uses the dividends you receive to purchase additional shares.

Creating a dividend strategy

A dividend growth approach tends to involve some combination of the following:

- Building a collection of great companies that increase their dividends at a rate equal to or substantially in excess of inflation each year.
- Holding on to positions for long periods, often decades, to take advantage of deferred taxes as it allows more capital to be working

for you, which means more dividends being pumped out for your family.

- Diversifying across different industries and sectors so your dividend stream isn't too reliant on a single area of the economy such as oil, banking, or mining.
- Making sure the dividend growth is being financed by higher levels of real underlying profit, not ever-expanding debt.

Which stock would you prefer for your portfolio?

- Stock A has a dividend yield of 3.00%. The board of directors has historically increased the dividend by 5% per annum and the dividend payout ratio currently stands at 60%.

- Stock B has a dividend yield of 0.50%. The company is growing rapidly to the point that 20%+ jumps in diluted EPS have not been uncommon over the past five years. The dividend is almost always increased accordingly. The stock currently has a dividend payout ratio of 10%.

If you follow the dividend growth investing strategy, you're probably going to opt for Stock B, all else being equal. It may seem counter-intuitive, but you will end up cashing larger aggregate dividend checks by owning it than you will Stock A, provided the growth can be maintained for a long enough stretch of time. As the earnings climb, and the dividend is increased alongside profits, your yield-on-cost starts to overtake the slower growing company.

Where can you learn more about individual dividend stocks?

You should access reputable sources for information about the companies issuing these stocks, their financial statements (such as the P/L), and associated dividend metrics (such as the payout ratio).

Financial news sites: These can be useful in gathering information about a company's current dividend yield while offering high quality, up-to-date data, tools, and analytics. Morningstar is an excellent resource for researching dividend data. You can also check out the Wall Street Journal, Investopedia, Bloomberg, MarketWatch, and CNBC.

Brokerage accounts: Many brokerage accounts offer online research and pricing information on their websites. They often offer personalized reports tied to your individual investor profile, as well.

Securities and Exchange Commission (SEC): The SEC keeps a record of the dividends paid by all publicly trading companies during the previous tax year on a quarterly and annual basis. Access these reports by visiting SEC.gov using their EDGAR system.

Stock exchanges: There are tools and resources available directly on stock exchanges themselves. For example, the New York Stock Exchange (NYSE) offers a historical database by which you can look up dividends for a selected date range.

Playing the long game

Investing with a long-term mindset allows you to focus on what really matters for long-term success. An additional benefit of long-term investing is a reduction in taxes and fees versus higher turnover strategies. With a well-thought-out dividend investment plan, you can grow your money in every season and experience steady cash flow and increasing returns when you reinvest your dividends.

Investing takes quite a bit of work. Do you have time to investigate and monitor all the companies you're investing in? Working with a professional can help ensure your portfolio aligns with your expectations by monitoring and making necessary adjustments. Financial advisory and investment firms have a lot more tools, systems, and risk controls at their disposal. In Chapter 7, I'll discuss investment advisors and how to choose the right individual or firm to work with.

But before I go into that, we need to discuss your risk profile. And we need to know how much risk you're willing to take in your portfolio and investment decisions.

How does this risk profile match up to your financial goals and planning? In the next chapter, let's take a closer look at your risk profile to understand how you can apply these investing strategies at a risk level that you're comfortable with.

Key takeaway

It's important to maximize your overall return — not just your covered call return. Expiration dates, varying strike prices, and knowing when not to write a covered call, are the keys to making that happen.

"An investment in knowledge pays the best interest."

- Benjamin Franklin, a writer, printer, political philosopher, Freemason, postmaster, scientist, inventor, humorist, civic activist, diplomat, and famous risk-seeker

I n the previous chapters, you've learned about covered calls and dividends, examined historical market data, and the essentials of how to invest using these strategies. Now, let's take a closer look at your own risk profile to understand how you can apply these investing strategies at a risk level that you're comfortable with. Determining your risk profile helps you mitigate risks and figure out the right investment asset allocation for your portfolio.

What is a risk profile?

A risk profile is essentially a method of determining the acceptable amount of risk that an individual is prepared to take. How much risk you're willing to take, or are averse to taking, affects your decision-making in terms of your asset allocation for your investment portfolio.

The spectrum of risk profiles ranges from risk-averse (less risk) to risk-seeker (more risk). Most people are somewhere in the middle and can lean in one direction or the other. When you're afraid of taking on risk that could cause a decline in the value of the portfolio, you're risk-averse. When you want to see larger gains and are willing to take on more risk, you're a risk-seeker.

Your risk profile is affected by your financial situation and ability to take on risk. If you have a lot of liabilities (debt) and little cash assets, you'll tend to be more risk-averse because you can't afford to take on risk. If you have large cash assets and few liabilities, you're better positioned to take on risk. Also, your willingness to take on risk is dependent on temperament and preferences. Building your portfolio is reliant upon both your ability to take on risk and your willingness to do so.

Gauging your risk profile

You can gauge your risk profile by answering essential questions about your risk tolerance, your assets, and your goals. Brokerage firms such as Schwab, Vanguard, and others provide free risk-profile questionnaires, based on fundamental investment principles. They don't serve to replace your existing financial strategy or provide you with comprehensive financial advice on their own. I almost always recommend working with a qualified financial professional. The answers to these questions provide knowledge into understanding your risk tolerance, which can be used to develop an investment portfolio best suited to you.

Risky business

Your ability to take on risk, and your willingness to do so, determine if you're risk-averse, a risk-seeker, or somewhere in between.

These investor profile questionnaires are a great starting point. They measure important factors: your time horizon and your risk tolerance.

Time horizon refers to the length of time of your investment. Will you be withdrawing cash from your account soon or at a later date? At what rate will you withdraw funds? If your account has more time to grow and you don't need access to the cash right away, your account will have more time to appreciate and to weather stock market ups and downs.

Your tolerance

How comfortable are you with risk? Some investments may have dramatic fluctuations in value with high potential for larger gains, while others may be more stable with lower returns. It's important that you choose investments that fit within your risk tolerance level.

Get an idea of your risk tolerance by answering these seven questions.

Sample seven-question investor profile questionnaire:

Time horizon

Circle the number of points for each of your answers and note the total for each section.

1. I want to start withdrawing money from my investments in:

Less than 3 years 1

3–5 years 3

6–10 years 7

11 years or more 10

2. As I start withdrawing money from my investments, my plan is to spend all the money in:

Less than 2 years 0

2–5 years 1

6–10 years 4

11 years or more 8

Your time horizon score = The total points from questions 1 and 2.

_____

If your time horizon scores below 3, you have a very short investment time horizon and don't need to continue the questionnaire. In this case, I recommend a relatively low-risk portfolio of 40% short-term (with an average maturity of five years or less) bonds or bond funds and 60% cash investments — stocks may be much more volatile in the short term. If you're score is 3 or more, continue answering the following questions.

Risk tolerance

3. My investment knowledge is:

None 1

Limited 3

Good 7

Extensive 10

4. When I invest, I'm concerned about:

My investment losing value 0

Wheterh my investment is losing or gaining value 4

My investment gaining value 8

5. Choose the investments you currently own:

Bonds and/or bond funds 3

Stocks and/or stock funds 6

International securities and/or international funds 8

Example: You own stock funds now but, in the past, you've bought international securities. Your score is 6.

6. What would you do in this scenario:

Imagine that in the past three months, the overall stock market lost 25% of its value. An individual stock investment you own also lost 25% of its value. What would you do?

Sell all of my shares 0

Sell some of my shares 2

Do nothing 5

Buy more shares 8

7. What range of outcomes suits you best?

The following hypothetical investment plans show best-case and worst-case annual returns. All figures are hypothetical and don't represent the performance of any particular investment. Which range of potential outcomes is most acceptable to you? The figures are hypothetical and do not represent the performance of any particular investment.

Plan	Avg. Annual Return	Best-case	Worst-case	Points
A	7.2%	16.3%	-5.6%	0
B	9.0%	24.0%	-12.1%	3
C	10.4%	33.6%	-18.2%	6
D	11.7%	42.8%	-24.0%	8
E	2.5%	50.0%	-28.2%	10

Enter the total points from questions 3 through 7. This is your risk tolerance score: _____

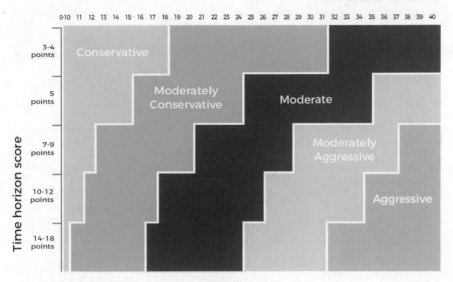

Determine your investor profile

Now you're going to use the above chart and the subtotals you calculated in the preceding two sections to determine your investor profile. Find your time horizon score along the left side and your risk tolerance score across the top. Locate their intersection point, situated in the area that corresponds to your investor profile.

From there, you can get an idea of which investment strategy corresponds with your investor profile. This is a great exercise to go through on your own before you meet with your financial advisor. It helps to ensure that you're all on the same page.

Select your investment strategy

The investment strategies on page 114 show how investors might allocate their money among investments in various categories. Please note that these examples aren't based on market forecasts, but simply reflect an established approach to investing — allocating dollars among different investment categories.

Keep in mind that it's important to periodically review your investment strategy to make sure it continues to be consistent with your goals.

BACKSTORY:

This is the biggest change I've seen in the business.

After the tech bubble burst and the market corrected, the digital age arrived and brought with it more access to information. Obviously, the ability to access everything on our phones was revolutionary — which was a far cry from having to share a Quotron machine with other trainees when I first got started in the business.

Back then, if you wanted to get a live stock quote, you could check the old-fashioned ticker tape, call the order clerk, or walk up to the front of the office to sit at the Quotron and type a quote. If you chose to leave the desk and walk up to check stock quotes, you had to prepare to be ridiculed since you weren't using your time to talk to clients.

If you were up there looking at the Quotron screen for too long, you'd be called a "boxwatcher." As a trainee, this was not a good thing. Eventually, someone would ask what I was doing up there. I would answer that I was looking at the market, only to hear, "How much of that market do ya got?" and echoing laughter.

The ability to have information flow so freely in the digital age is such a juxtaposition to when it felt like a privilege to get a stock quote when I was learning the business. This access to information and sources makes people smarter and allows you to

make better decisions as an investor.

This change improved the quality of life for people in the investment world and gave clients transparency to see what their portfolios were doing and where potential risks existed. That is incredibly important — it helps create authenticity and makes all of us better.

Access and the ability to bring down the commodity cost of trading has improved performance for portfolio managers.

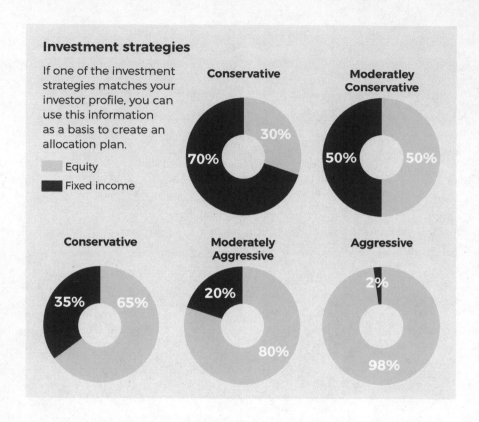

Investment strategies

If one of the investment strategies matches your investor profile, you can use this information as a basis to create an allocation plan.

- Equity
- Fixed income

Conservative
30%
70%

Moderatley Conservative
50% 50%

Conservative
35% 65%

Moderately Aggressive
20%
80%

Aggressive
2%
98%

A deeper approach to your investor profile

Financial advisors use a more comprehensive investor profile questionnaire as part of their planning process. This helps financial advisors determine the risk capacity and risk willingness of their clients, and helps them map clients to recommended individual portfolios. In this risk profile questionnaire, you answer more detailed questions about your goals, time horizon, and risk profile. This type of analysis helps you and your financial advisor.

Upon completion, you receive a portfolio recommendation that matches your portfolio risk level.

Modern financial planning utilizes two independent and separate risk scores: risk capacity and risk willingness. A majority of risk tolerance questionnaires focus only on risk capacity, which offers insight into your ability to handle risk.

You also need to provide information about your willingness to take on risk. Behavioral questions on risk willingness provide insight into how investors behave in practice rather than in theory alone.

This do-it-yourself approach is a good start, but it doesn't replace working with a qualified financial professional. Financial planners help to connect the emotional dots of risk analysis.

Measuring behavioral insights in three essential areas:

- **Capacity to take risks.** Some questions capture factual information used to calculate a risk capacity score. Risk capacity is based on factual information about your investment objective, initial investment amount, and time horizon.

- **Willingness to take risks and attitude toward risk.** Other questions collect information about your behavioral attitude toward risk, and the answers are used to calculate a risk willingness score. Risk willingness indicates how willing you are to accept investment risk in terms of volatility of investment returns as well as the probability of loss.

> **Understanding yourself**
>
> A more thorough approach to your risk profile will get to the heart of why you may act one way when you think you might do the opposite. This is behavioral finance.

- **Investment preferences.** Additional questions can be asked to capture information about your age and investment preferences, such as income profile, tax-loss harvesting, and charitable inclinations. The age question is asked to help determine the validity of prior responses. Other questions are only asked if you choose portfolios that require these features. The answers to these questions aren't used to determine risk scores but are helpful in determining the appropriate investment strategy and types of potential portfolios to choose from.

Scoring

Both the risk capacity and risk willingness questions are scored and totaled separately. In typical surveys, each risk dimension has a maximum of 100 points. Higher scores indicate a higher level of risk capacity or risk willingness, and you're mapped to a risk profile based on their total scores for each risk dimension. This risk profile is then used to suggest an appropriate portfolio.

Risk capacity score

Questions about time horizon influence this score considerably because time horizon is one of the key deciding factors of whether your portfolio will be able to withstand volatile periods.

Your goal is the second most important question in determining the risk capacity score because different goals have different levels of importance.

Risk willingness score

Questions in this risk dimension consist of quantifiable situational questions, which carry more weight, and simple introspective questions. Quantifiable situational questions put you in actual situations where you have to choose, while the introspective questions are informative and subjective.

These types of questionnaires are geared toward achieving one client-focused goal, so if you wanted to achieve multiple financial goals, you would use the same process for each individual goal and map out corresponding portfolio asset allocations.

These insights add context to the questionnaire on page 109:

Insight 1: Investment goal (risk capacity)

Addresses the primary goal of having this investment account. For example, a goal such as saving for a vacation can handle more risk than essential goals such as an emergency fund. Some goals such as retirement are very important but also take considerable time to complete.

Insight 2: Investment knowledge (risk willingness)

Helps to determine your knowledge of investments and how comfortable you are with investing. Often, when a client understands investments, they are willing to accept more risk. This often happens because the client understands that higher risk can come with higher rewards, and that investing includes periods of volatility and decline.

Insight 3: Risk perception (risk willingness)

Helps define a client's attitude toward the word "risk." How you perceive risk is important because you want to make asset allocations that you are comfortable with, even if you have a capacity to take on more risk.

After you answer the questions, your investment advisor will map out an investment portfolio from your profile. It's important to go through this exercise with your financial professional on an ongoing basis because your financial goals and your tolerance for risk will surely change over time.

How clients are mapped to portfolios

During this process, each response is scored and then used to calculate the score totals for the risk capacity and risk willingness. Your advisor then uses a grid to map out a specific portfolio for you. This extra step enhances traditional risk tolerance questionnaires by giving insight into your financial situation and attitude toward risk. Goals and time horizon affect the scoring.

Evaluating risk factors

Investment involves risk — have I mentioned that enough yet? It's important that you figure out what those risks might be, which ones you are willing to take, and which ones may never be worth taking.

Use these three approaches to assess risk:

• Determine the kind of risk you're comfortable taking.

> **Willing and able**
>
> Your capacity and willingness to take on risk are both key dimensions to help determine one, focused investing goal.

• Understand the risk posed by certain categories of investments.

• Evaluate specific investments.

You can determine this on your own or with the help of an investment professional.

Selecting risk

While it's rare to avoid investment risk entirely, determining the level of risk that is appropriate for you and your situation can be helpful in managing your risk exposure. There are three essential factors in selecting your risk:

• Your goals and your timeline for meeting them.

• Your financial responsibilities.

• Your other financial resources.

Understanding types of risks

Risk is a term frequently used in financial discussions, but often misunderstood.

Often when people talk about risk in the media, they usually focus on the historical price volatility of a specific asset or investment. Advisors call an investment aggressive or risky when it has experienced big price fluctuations in the past. Assets that have a smaller and narrower range of ups (peaks) and downs (valleys) are considered conservative. Still, this isn't clearly explained in the media or on TV, and often the feedback you're getting can be disconcerting and incomplete.

Every investment carries risk, with a possible loss of principal or buying power. There's no guarantee that any investment strategy will be successful. Yet, a well-constructed investment portfolio remains one of the most successful ways to grow your asset base. It helps to understand the kinds of risk and the extent of risk that you choose to take, and then to learn ways to manage those risks.

In addition to volatility, there are other types of risk, described here:

Market risk: The possibility that an investment will lose value because of a general decline in financial markets due to economic, political, or other factors.

Inflation risk: Refers to the possibility that prices will rise in the economy as a whole due to inflation, and your ability to purchase goods and services with your investment dollars would decline. For example, if your investment yielded a 6% return, but the inflation rate rose to double digits, the invested dollars would buy less than the same dollars today.

Interest rate risk: Relates to increases or decreases in prevailing interest rates and the resulting price fluctuation of an investment, particularly bonds. There's an inverse relationship between bond prices and interest rates. As interest rates rise, the price of bonds falls. As interest rates fall, bond prices tend to rise. If you need to sell your bond before it matures and your principal is returned, you run the risk of losing the principal if interest rates are higher than when you purchased the bond.

Reinvestment rate risk: The possibility that you'll have to reinvest funds at a lower rate of return than your original investment. For example, your five-year, 3.75% certificate of deposit might mature at a time when a new certificate of deposit pays just 3%.

Default risk: Refers to the possibility that a bond issuer won't be able to pay their bondholders' interest or repay principal.

Liquidity risk: Refers to how quickly your investments can be converted to cash.

Political risk: This refers to the possibility that new legislation or changes in foreign governments will adversely affect financial markets overseas or companies you invest in.

Currency risk: This refers to the possibility that the fluctuating rates of exchange between U.S. and foreign currencies will negatively affect the value of your foreign investment, as measured in U.S. dollars.

Volatility risk

Here's a hypothetical example to help explain volatility.

Let's say you invested $10,000 in two mutual funds 20 years ago, and that the average annual return of both was 10%.

The Slow & Steady Fund gave you a 10% return every year.

The Zip Zip Hare Fund had alternating years, with 5% up one year, 15% the next, and so on.

How much would each of these investments be worth at the end of 20 years? Despite investing the same amount over the same period, these two funds could have differing returns on their investments. The Slow & Steady Fund could've performed better than Zip Zip Hare Fund. The difference increases if the annual variations in Zip Zip Hare Fund are larger. Short-term fluctuations can affect long-term growth and the effect of investment price volatility — short-term fluctuations in returns could be a drag on long-term growth.

The negative effect and risk of having short-term price fluctuations is lowered by holding investments over longer periods. This helps you ride out the ups and downs of the investment cycle. Doing this would require more planning. If you need funds in the near future, you shouldn't be investing in a volatile investment, or you might lose money if you had to sell the investment for cash purposes.

How risk and reward work

Typically, the more risk that you're willing to take on, the higher your potential returns and potential losses are. People take on high-risk investments because of the potential rewards of receiving higher returns. That's why financial professionals focus on risk-adjusted returns. Your goal must be to maximize returns without taking on too much risk.

Your tolerance for risk depends on your risk capacity and your risk willingness. It's also affected by your age, stage in life, and goals. If you're investing for retirement and are 45 years old, you're at a different stage in life than someone who is 65 and ready to retire. You have more time to grow your money and to earn more, and hence can take on more risk.

When you have 30 years to build a nest egg, your investments have more time to ride out short-term fluctuations with the hope of receiving a greater long-term return.

Avenues to assess risk

You can assess risks by becoming more informed about a prospective investment before you invest. Talk to your advisor, and check out third-party business and financial publications, websites that provide credit ratings, news stories, and a company's annual reports.

You can also obtain a prospectus if the investment is a mutual fund, ETF, or is in an initial public offering (IPO). The prospectus contains information about the company's products and services, operating history, future prospects, and management. The offering circular of a limited partnership or hedge fund also contains information similar to that of a prospectus for an IPO, including the general partner, special risks of investing in the product, and liquidity.

The Securities and Exchange Commission (SEC) also has information about events such as large stock sales, purchases, mergers, acquisitions, and financial reports.

Company documents

Every public company has to register its securities with the SEC and provide updated information on a periodic basis. The annual report on Form 10-K contains audited financial statements and detailed information about the company, the people who run it, and the risks of investing in the company. Companies also submit three additional quarterly reports called 10-Qs and interim reports on Form 8-K to the

SEC, which are available using the SEC's EDGAR database.

Rating services

Independent rating services such as Moody's offer independent information about specific corporate and municipal bonds that you may own or may be considering. Each rating company has different steps for evaluation, but all focus on the issuer's ability to meet its financial promises and obligations. The higher the letter grade a rating company assigns, the lower the risk you take. Ratings aren't perfect, but they do provide some insight on the company. Traditionally, the SEC has a list of rating agencies on its website.

Research reports

As we mentioned, companies such as financial firms and independent research providers give detailed research reports to rate stocks, mutual funds, and other investments.

Mitigating risk

Now that you understand the essentials of how to assess risk, it's important to learn how to mitigate or reduce your investment risk. History has shown that when people stay invested over the long term, they are more likely to earn positive returns. When markets fluctuate, you may feel tempted to react and make financial decisions and change your portfolio. However, people who base their financial decisions on emotion often end up buying when the market is high and selling when prices are low, and struggle to meet their long-term financial goals.

You can mitigate risk with these investment strategies:

1. Be cautious when making an investment decision based on a short-term gain or loss.

2. Review your asset allocation and diversification strategies to ensure your risk and reward levels align with your long-term investment goals.

3. Consider dollar-cost averaging to help smooth out the effect of market volatility over time, and help eliminate emotional upheavals from your financial decisions.

Strategy 1: Asset allocation

Asset allocation is how you weigh investments in your portfolio to meet a specific objective. This decision has a large effect on the success of your financial goals. Before you decide how to divide the asset classes in your portfolio, it's important that you review your timeframe and the risks and rewards of each asset class.

Stocks typically carry a higher level of risk over the short term due to fluctuating markets. They also tend to earn higher long-term returns than other asset classes, and usually outpace inflation over the long term. Bonds have fewer short-term price fluctuations than stocks and therefore have lower market risk.

Bonds preserve the safety of your principal, offer lower long-term returns, and incur higher inflation risks over time. As I mentioned, bond prices typically fall when interest rates rise. Money market funds are stable in terms of asset classes with lower market risk, but can't outpace inflation.

Air time

Need more Kevin? You can catch him sharing his expertise as a guest on CNBC, Yahoo Finance, or you can subscribe to his popular podcast.

As you can see, different asset classes have different levels of potential return and market risk. Past performance doesn't mean that future results are the same. Asset allocations also don't guarantee a profit.

Strategy 2: Portfolio diversification

You can reduce your risk through portfolio diversification. This goes hand in hand with asset allocation and helps you offset some of the risk of any single investment by spreading your money among several asset classes. Diversification strategies leverage the fact that market forces typically don't affect all types or classes of investment assets at the same time or in the same way. By diversifying your investments among assets that are not highly correlated and behave differently, you stand a better chance of mitigating risk.

While diversification can't guarantee a profit or ensure against loss, it can help you manage the level and types of risk you face.

You can diversify among asset classes and within them. Diversifying within an asset class helps you reduce the impact on your portfolio of any one type of stock, bond, or mutual fund. If you invest in the stock of just one company, you take on greater risk by relying on the performance of a single stock to grow your investment.

However, if you invest in 20 - 25 companies in different industries, you can reduce the possibility of having a substantial loss. While one investment value may go down, another may go up, potentially offsetting some of the loss of the investment that isn't performing well.

Strategy 3: Dollar-cost averaging

Dollar-cost averaging is a disciplined investment strategy to help you smooth out the wrinkles of market fluctuations in your portfolio. Here, you apply a specific dollar amount toward the purchase of stocks, bonds, and mutual funds on a regular basis.

You purchase more shares when prices are low and fewer shares when prices are high. The average cost of your shares will usually be lower than the average price of those shares over time. This process is systematic and can help you avoid making emotionally based investment decisions.

Here's an example of how dollar-cost averaging could work in both rising and declining markets. This example is for an investment between $10 and $25, January through April. By investing a fixed monthly amount of $100, you can buy as many as 10 shares when the price is at its lowest ($10 each), but only four shares when the price is highest ($25 each). In this example, dollar-cost averaging results in a lower average share price during the period, while the market average price for an individual who bought the same number of shares per month is higher.

Rising market

Dollar-cost averaging at $100 per month.

Month	When the price is ...	You buy
January	$10	10.00 shares
February	$15	6.67 shares
March	$20	5.00 shares
April	$25	4.00 shares

Declining market

Dollar-cost averaging at $100 per month

Month	When the price is ...	You buy
January	$25	4.00 shares
February	$20	5.00 shares
March	$10	10.00 shares
April	$5	20.00 shares

Risk protection

In addition to your due diligence and the advice of your investment advisor, you also have access to information and support from several federal, state, and private-sector agencies. These organizations help ensure that you have sufficient information to make investment decisions, protect against specific losses, and provide oversight for the companies and individuals that you invest in.

SEC: While the SEC doesn't evaluate investments or profits, it does provide detailed financial information about all publicly traded companies and information on how the company operates, its management team, and the risks posed. The SEC also can investigate companies that issue registered securities, advisors that recommend those securities, investment companies (mutual funds) that sell them, and take legal action against any of them. The SEC also oversees credit rating agencies that evaluate bond issuers.

NASAA: State securities regulators are part of a nationwide organization called the North American Securities Administrators Association (NASAA) and register securities that are sold only within their state borders. They license brokers, brokerage firms, and small investment adviser firms (managing $100 million or less in assets) that do business in their states. When an investment adviser has more than $110 million under management, it must register with the SEC. State regulators help protect investors against fraud.

FINRA: The Financial Industry Regulatory Authority (FINRA) is the largest, non-governmental self-regulatory organization for the securities industry. It operates under the jurisdiction of the SEC. FINRA helps oversee the activities of brokerage firms (broker-dealers and registered representatives). FINRA also checks communications from member brokerage firms to ensure that the information is accurate, not misleading, clearly explains risks and rewards, and provides full disclosure of any conflicts of interest. FINRA can also investigate and discipline firms.

FINRA also maintains a service called BrokerCheck that reviews the employment history, disciplinary record, and qualifications of brokers and brokerage firms, as well as investment advisers and investment adviser firms. You can check out a broker or brokerage firm to help you avoid the risk of working with an unregistered person or firm, and you can learn about prior disciplinary histories or customer complaints. This useful information is available on FINRA's website at www.finra.org/brokercheck.

SIPC: The Securities Investor Protection Corporation (SIPC) is a nonprofit, non-government membership corporation that is funded by member broker-dealers and provides limited protections to investors. If a firm that clears securities trades is financially incapable of returning the customer's property, it's SIPC's responsibility to make sure the customer's cash and securities are returned within limits specified by law. The SIPC doesn't protect against market risk, but does offer limited protection against unauthorized trading in customers' securities accounts.

Choose the right approach

After learning all the potential pitfalls, it's understandable that you might be wondering why take any risk at all. There are times when you don't want to put any money at risk, such as saving for your emergency fund, planning for medical expenses, education, your home, or other essential expenses for which you need immediate access to cash. However, beyond these needs, your money needs to cover your long-term goals.

Investing comes with risk, but also opens the door to greater returns and the potential to earn dividends or interest on your investments. Also, the

Industry watchdogs

SEC: You can file a complaint via the SEC website or by calling 800-SEC-0330 (800-732-0330).

NASAA: Visit www.nasaa.org or call 202-737-0900, or write to NASAA, 750 First St., NE, Suite 1140, Washington, DC, 20002.

FINRA: Contact the FINRA Call Center at 301-590-6500. FINRA has a toll-free line for senior investors: 844-574-3577.

SIPC: Visit sipc.org or call 202-371-8300.

value of the assets you purchase may increase over the longer term.

Now that you know the types of risk, how to protect against risk, where to learn more about investment opportunities, and your own risk tolerance, you're more prepared to create an investment portfolio that is right for you. One of the best ways to manage risk is to build a diversified portfolio that holds different types of investments. This helps mitigate risk because some of your investments will increase in value over a period of time, while others decrease.

Remember, the rate of your investment growth will outpace returns from placing your cash in a risk-free insured bank savings that often can't keep up with inflation and doesn't grow your money significantly.

Key takeaway

Building your portfolio is dependent both upon your ability to take on risk and your willingness to do so.

"Trust is the glue of life. It's the most essential ingredient in effective communication. It's the foundational principle that holds all relationships."

- Stephen Covey, American educator, author, businessman, and keynote speaker

We're stating the obvious here, but investment advisors help you decide how to best manage your money and achieve your financial goals. Each individual is different, though, and a one-size-fits-all approach doesn't work. You have many options, and here are four of them: broker/stockbroker, Registered Investment Advisor (RIA), Certified Financial Planner (CFP), and online robo-advisor.

In addition, there are specialty services and concentrations such as Chartered Financial Analysts (CFAs). There are also enrolled agents focused solely on tax preparation. Finally, you can work with wealth managers who concentrate on providing investment services for high-net-worth clients.

Four primary types of investment advisors

Broker or stockbroker: Person or company that purchases and sells financial products on behalf of clients for a commission, fee, or both. To be a broker or stockbroker, the person has to pass specific exams and register with the U.S. Securities and Exchange Commission.

Registered Investment Advisor: Person or company that provides financial investment advice and offers recommendations for a fee. RIAs are registered with the U.S. Securities and Exchange Commission or a state regulator. RIAs vary in their focus and expertise, and some focus solely on investment portfolios, while others provide a comprehensive suite of financial planning services.

Certified Financial Planner: Person or company that offers financial planning advice. To become a CFP, the person needs to fulfill an extensive education requirement, pass a precise and rigorous exam, and demonstrate sufficient work experience.

Robo-advisor: An online service or mobile app that employs computer software and algorithms to manage investment portfolios.

What's the right fit for you?

Now that you know the types of investment advisors, the next step is to determine your essential requirements. This boils down to three primary aspects: services, costs, and qualifications.

Services

What kind of investment advisory help do you want? Are you looking for simple investment management or do you want a more hands-on approach where you are very involved in the process? Do you want comprehensive financial planning services? Determining what you need and want is the first and most important step in figuring out the right type of investment advisor for you.

Costs

How much does the service cost? What are the fees involved? Is the financial advisor paid a commission, fee, or both?

Qualifications

What are the qualifications of your investment advisor? If you're hiring an investment firm, what certifications does the company have? Is it registered with the SEC?

For example, you could have a robo-advisor or mobile app if you're just starting out and want a streamlined, automatic, and cost-efficient process. Robo-advisory services often have low or zero account minimum-balance requirements. If you're looking for more comprehensive financial planning services for your retirement, planning your retirement, meeting insurance needs, or other personal goals, you'd benefit from working with an individual advisor who is either an RIA or CFP. You can also do both, starting with an online advisor so you can benefit from stock market gains immediately, and then add the services of an RIA as a next step for more comprehensive investment planning.

In terms of fees, online advisory fees range from 0 - 0.75% of the assets managed for you. Individual advisors typically charge a fee that is a percentage of the amount being managed, usually around 1 - 1.5%. Some advisory firms require a minimum asset value, as well, such as $250,000, to be managed. Some investment advisors charge a flat fee, retainer, or hourly rate. It's best to check fees prior to making a commitment to an individual or firm.

Fee considerations

Be sure to review how you're going to be charged for services. Fees can be a percentage of assets being managed, a flat fee, retainer, or hourly rate.

Another layer of protection

To determine the qualifications and standards of any company or individual advisor you're thinking of hiring, you can check their records. The most important document to check is Form ADV.

Form ADV is a disclosure document filed with the SEC and state securities authorities. This filing is required for all investment advisory professionals including robo-advisory service providers online. Typically, you can receive a free copy through the Investment Adviser Public Disclosure's website at www.advisorinfo.sec.gov. You can also check local state regulatory filings where your financial advisor operates by visiting the NASAA website at www.nasaa.org/about-us/contact-us/contact-your-regulator/.

Form ADV contains details such as the full business name, resume, description of services offered, types and numbers of clients served, the

BACKSTORY:

It's fun and easy to buy stocks. It's really hard to know when to sell them.

It's exciting when you make an investment in a stock. I see it all the time. It's thrilling at the start, but then those emotions give way and strategy sets in — because you don't want to be wrong. You start thinking about if and when to sell the stock.

If the stock goes up, you don't sell because, of course, what if it goes higher? But what if the stock goes down? How can you possibly sell a stock that's down? Maybe you wait for the stock to come back to break even. But if it does, you're probably won't sell now because you waited so long for it to come back up.

I know how confusing it can get. It's impossible to consistently know how to sell a stock if you're a retail investor. I know many, many wealthy and successful investors, but only a handful of wealthy and successful traders.

That's why I try to remove emotion from the process and stick to the rules of a Sell Discipline when managing portfolios. I use these four principles when deciding whether to sell a stock:

Follow the 5% rule. If we own a company, we cap it at 5% of the portfolio — no matter what it is. If the company grows, and becomes 7 or 8%, the casino impulse can kick in to let it ride. It's key to rebalance the portfolio by trimming the position back to 5%, taking the profit, and reallocating the proceeds.

Cut companies that cut dividends. While companies don't always have to raise dividends, we sell a stock when they cut their dividend.

Sell for specific underperformance. If a stock we own underperforms its peer group or sector by 15 - 20%, something is happening at the company level. There is a reason for the underperformance, that we may not figure out until later, but we remove it from the portfolio as soon as possible to avoid further declines.

Meet contractual obligations. Sometimes with covered call writing, we're contractually obligated to sell a stock (as I talked about in Chapter 3).

Remember, I believe in only owning dividend-paying stocks to begin with. If the stock doesn't move up or down, it can still pay a dividend and enhance income. At CWP, we insist on getting paid while we wait — you should, too.

amount of assets managed, a brief company history, certifications, education, and the work history of the principals. It also contains an explanation of the advisor fees and billing practices. Form ADV also shares information about disciplinary actions (regulatory and judicial) that may have been taken against the individual or company.

Work with someone you trust

Your financial investment advisor is someone you'll be working with for a long time, and they will know everything about your finances. It's important to choose a person and/or company that you feel comfortable with and confident in trusting their decisions. You're essentially entering a long-term relationship that's similar to dating — you need to be compatible, work well together, and be comfortable planning goals and dealing with problems along the way. An important aspect of establishing trust is learning about your investment advisor's approach and if the individual adheres by the fiduciary rule.

What is the fiduciary standard?

Before we get into the rule, let's explore the standard. According to the Investment Advisers Act of 1940, investment advisors are bound to a fiduciary standard where financial advisors must put client interests above their own. This practice can be enforced and regulated by both the SEC and local state security regulators. Following this standard has the biggest impact upon brokers and insurance agents.

Acting in your best interest

The fiduciary rule was a rule established by the Department of Labor in 2016 that dictates that financial advisors need to act in the best interest of their clients and above their own. This rule is awaiting final approval, but many advisory firms have already adopted this practice.

The fiduciary rule expands upon an existing 1940 fiduciary standard that was later defined in the Employee Retirement Income Security Act of 1974 (ERISA). The 1940 standard came out of a Massachusetts legal decision that occurred 90 years prior, Harvard College vs. Armory, that defined the obligations of a fiduciary as a person who is responsible for managing money on someone else's behalf. That led to the adoption of the

Prudent Man Rule, which states that people in charge of another individual's money must manage that money with the care and skill they would do if it were their own.

What is a fiduciary?

A fiduciary is a person or a legal entity (brokerage firm or bank) that has the power and responsibility to act in the best interest of another individual or entity, called the beneficiary or principal. Given that fiduciaries have the power to make financial decisions on behalf of beneficiaries, it's important that fiduciaries are trustworthy and honest. Fiduciary duties extend beyond financial management. They also apply to a trustee, a trust, corporate officers managing a public corporation, and attorneys and real estate agents who have fiduciary duties to their clients.

In terms of investments, fiduciaries can buy and sell securities on behalf of beneficiaries without needing to check in or get express consent prior to each trade from the beneficiaries. Since fiduciaries are entrusted with such discretionary power, they're held to a higher standard than non-fiduciary advisors are.

The highest standard of care

According to the Cornell Law Dictionary, "A fiduciary duty is the highest standard of care." This means that a fiduciary must always act in the best interest of the beneficiary, even if that means recommending a product that doesn't provide the fiduciary with immediate compensation, because that's the best option for the client.

The way the SEC sees it, fiduciary duty involves acting with undivided loyalty and utmost good faith, providing fair and full disclosure of all material facts, defined as what "a reasonable investor would consider to be important not misleading clients, avoiding any conflict of interest, and not using a client's assets for someone else's benefit or for the advisor's own benefit."

The SEC ends with the statement that "departure from this fiduciary standard may constitute 'fraud' upon your clients," all of which can result in multi-million-dollar penalties, revoking a firm's or investment advisor's registration, barring the advisor from the industry, and other judgments.

Many people implicitly trust that their advisors are acting in their best

BACKSTORY:

Measure success by how well you do in periods of high volatility and market declines.

In my 30 years as a professional, I now realize it's not always easy to see a market crash coming. How you handle It Is what matters. How you manage portfolios during periods of high volatility and corrections is how you gain your mettle as a portfolio manager. It becomes an experience of knowing what to do, instead of focusing on what might have caused it.

I'm really proud of how we fared at Capital Wealth Planning in 2008 and 2020 during those voracious declines. Like I tell my son, "Anyone can make money when the ticker and the stock market are going up." I'm not suggesting we were always profitable or made money during those declines, but we were able to limit the losses. That, to me, is the measure of success.

interest as fiduciaries, but that's not necessarily the case. Non-fiduciary advisors operate via a "suitability standard" instead of fiduciary standard, which is a lower standard of care.

What is the suitability rule?

FINRA created a suitability rule (FINRA Rule 2111) that brokers and brokerage firms must deal with customers in a fair way where they recommend "suitable" products to their customers.

The difference between a fiduciary and suitability standard

A suitability standard requires advice to be "suitable," where the financial professional has reason to offer a recommendation to the client for financial investment or financial situation. The advisor only needs to have adequate information to provide this advice. The primary difference between a fiduciary advisor and a non-fiduciary advisor acting under a suitability standard is the process of decision-making. Fiduciaries have to follow a process to determine their client's best interest and then after offering recommendations to their clients, they must fully explain their reasoning and ensure that their clients fully understand why they recommend such solutions.

> **Your best interest?**
>
> The suitability standard opens you up to a potential conflict of interest between what's best for you as a client, and what's best for your non-fiduciary advisor.

Financial advisors who operate under the suitability standard aren't required to have such a depth of conversation, nor are they obligated to monitor their client accounts or understand the overall financial picture of their clients. Their responsibilities and ties to the client's investments cease right after they place the initial trade. Suitability standards don't require that the advisor acts in the client's best interest but only that they ask for fair dealing with proper material information disclosure, reasonable pricing in relation to the market, disclosure of any conflict of interest, and prompt execution of orders with "reasonable diligence."

Non-fiduciary advisors aren't required to put their clients' best interests before their own. This means they can direct you to buy "suitable" products that help them earn more money through commissions as long as these products are in the range of suitable products for you.

So, a non-fiduciary advisor can recommend a more expensive investment with more fees, which means they earn more, even if you, the client, pay more and this investment isn't in your best interests. Given that their compensation structure is tied to commissions, it's difficult for the non-fiduciary advisor to not have some conflict of interest with what's best for the investor.

Since fiduciary advisors are legally bound to act in the client's best interest and operate on an asset-management fee schedule without commissions, they are viewed as having fewer conflicts of interest than brokers are.

Now that you understand the different types of advisors and the three essential aspects to consider when choosing an investment advisor, it's important to interview your investment advisor before committing. Here are 10 questions to help you choose the right professional to work with.

10 questions to ask when selecting your investment advisor

Consider asking these questions during the interview process to help you understand the advisor's approach and whether they're the right fit for you.

1. Are you a fiduciary?

As mentioned earlier, fiduciary advisors work in the best interest of the client, whereas non-fiduciary advisors only have to recommend products that are deemed "suitable."

2. How do you get paid?

The financial industry is known for having multiple fees and commissions. It's best to know what you're paying up front to avoid unpleasant surprises, and I recommend working with an investment professional who charges a fee instead of commission. Then it's clear what you're paying. It could be a flat fee, hourly rate, retainer, or percentage of your assets. A 1-1.5% fee is common. Also, check if there is a minimum-investment amount. Some advisors will only work with high-net-worth individuals, and others have a minimum investment threshold. When you're first starting out, it's best to work with an advisor who doesn't have a required minimum investment threshold. Two networks that can help you in finding advisors without minimum requirements are the Garrett Planning Network and the National Association of Personal Financial Advisors. Remember, you can simply ask the investment professional you're considering working with, as well.

3. What are my costs?

In addition to paying your advisor, you will have other fees, and you'll want to know what these are. An analysis by the NerdWallet site discovered that a 1% mutual fund fee can cost as much as $590,000 in retirement savings to a millennial investor. It's important to not pay too much in add-on fees. Pay attention and ask about the fees you're paying.

4. What services do you include?

Does the investment professional offer the services you need? Are you looking for assistance with retirement planning, comprehensive financial planning services, tax advice, investment management, or some combination of these services? Does your investment advisor work with clients similar to you and will they be able to help you achieve your financial goals?

5. How do we communicate?

It's important that you know what type of access you'll have to your advisor. Do you meet in person, on Zoom, on the phone, or a combination? And how frequently?

6. What's your investment philosophy?

It's essential that you and your investment advisor are on the same page and have a similar investment philosophy.

7. What asset allocation will you use?

Asset allocation helps you create a diversified portfolio. Your portfolio must not be solely focused on just one stock or one set of stocks. Instead, your portfolio must be diversified and could include domestic and international stocks, small-cap, midcap, and large-cap companies. Your financial advisor must be comfortable discussing this with you.

8. Who is your custodian?

Some financial advisors work with a major institution (considered a custodian), such as Raymond James, Janney, LPL, or Morgan Stanley, which hold customers' securities to minimize the risk of theft or loss. If not, they'll partner with an independent custodian, such as a brokerage firm like Schwab or Fidelity to hold your investments, rather than act as their own custodian. This provides you with more security and safety. You need to know where your money is.

9. What investment benchmarks do you use?

Your investment advisor measures your portfolio performance against industry benchmarks. There are various benchmarks that can be used, and how they are used must make logical sense. For example, if your advisor uses the S&P 500 benchmark, that makes sense when considering investments in similar stocks, but you will need another benchmark to evaluate a diversified portfolio that contains emerging markets and small-cap stocks.

10. What taxes will I have to pay?

This helps you ensure that your investment advisor thinks about your tax payment when offering you financial advice. Your bottom line is to keep more money after fees and taxes are paid.

Finally, remember that your investment advisor must be willing to answer your questions and welcome the interaction. This is a long-term relationship, and you want to choose a capable, trustworthy person and/ or company that you feel comfortable working with and feel confident in their decision-making skills. It helps if you can speak to at least three potential advisors before making your decision.

On a last note, remember that your investment advisor is there to help you make sense of your financial life and guide you along the way. You'll want to work with someone who is polite and considerate. You're paying to get trustworthy financial guidance from a capable, intelligent, and honest person. Choose wisely.

Key takeaway

Knowing your overall goals, and what you want and need out of a financial planner or investment advisor, is a key step in selecting the right fit for a beneficial relationship.

"The best way to get started is to quit talking and begin doing."

- Walt Disney, an entrepreneur, animator, writer, voice actor, and film producer

I hope you've found this book useful and that it helps you start your walk toward a wealthy future. You've learned the essentials of covered calls and dividends, how to select a capable investment advisor, how to research and learn about stocks, bonds, ETFs, and mutual funds, and you know the importance of building an investment portfolio that matches your risk profile.

You also know the difference between investing and speculating, despite ads on TV or online encouraging you to speculate instead of invest. You know how to keep growing your wealth through covered calls and dividends, and you know how to prepare for inflation changes, higher interest rates, and increases in taxes.

You also understand how a dividend-focused portfolio that is tied to cash payments can be a buffer during periods of market volatility. You're ready to get started on building your investment portfolio using these time-tested, proven, and effective strategies.

You can do this on your own or hire a professional. Given the time requirements to research, make adjustments, strategize for dividend growth, and select the right investments for your portfolio, you may want to hire a professional to help — there are many skilled investment firms and individual professionals who can provide you with the necessary guidance. Our approach at Capital Wealth Planning (CWP) is outlined below, and I've included information about our Enhanced Dividend Income Portfolio (EDIP), which has a five-star overall Morningstar Rating (as of June 30, 2021).

Who we are

Capital Wealth Planning, LLC (CWP) is an SEC-registered fee-only investment advisory firm based in Naples, Florida. Building and managing proprietary income-oriented equity portfolios since 2005, the boutique firm has more than $4 billion of assets under management. The firm's methodologies are designed to enhance risk-adjusted returns and offer a modest portfolio protection while delivering monthly cash flow. Ranked by Financial Advisor Magazine in 2018, 2019, 2020, and 2021 as one of the top 50 fastest growing SEC-registered investment advisors in the country, CWP leads the implementation of covered call strategies with our Enhanced Dividend Income Portfolio (EDIP), ESG Enhanced Dividend Income Portfolio, ETF Covered Call Portfolio and Covered Call Overlay Transition Service. The firm also sub-advises on Amplify's Enhanced Dividend Income ETF (DIVO).

Our approach

At CWP, we realize the value of adapting to changes in markets and environments. We specialize in providing financial advisors with covered-call strategies. This allows our firm to focus solely on what we do best: Reduce risk and increase the yield of your portfolio. CWP is at the forefront of implementing covered-call strategies with our Enhanced Dividend Income Portfolios. We offer time-tested conservative strategies using covered-call writing designed to enhance income and overall total return.

Fee-based

Capital Wealth Planning is an independent, fee-only investment advisory firm registered with the SEC. CWP provides sub-advisory investment services to financial advisors, pensions, profit-sharing plans, trusts, estates, charitable organizations, and corporations.

The Three R's strategy behind EDIP

As with most things, exceptional and predictable results are invariably fueled by unique, strict, and structured discipline.

The specific strategy behind Capital Wealth Planning's Enhanced Dividend Income Portfolio (EDIP) is no exception, and is formally referred to as the Three R's – Rules, Risk, and Returns™.

Every decision to invest or not to invest is based on this strategy.

Rules

Regardless of where the market stands (up, down, or horizontal) rules must always follow in an unchanged progression to achieve the desired results. While some variables, changes, and inconsistencies arise, a rules-based strategy should remain fixed and revolve around how stocks are selected or sold. Investment in high-quality companies with strong balance sheets, great free cash flow, and good earnings and dividends is the first part of this high-payoff equation.

Consideration is also given for how the company and its market sector fit into the diversified portfolio being offered. The rules also apply to how a stock is sold, whether it's underperforming or overperforming.

Those rules combined with the defined strategy, play a tremendous role in how and when covered calls are written. Covered calls are not written for every investment at all times, but only those which will fit the strategy to mitigate risk while maximizing profits within a predictable range.

It's important to remember that a good rules-based strategy will always trade on mathematics and sound fundamentals, not emotions. At CWP, we believe that by separating emotions from the rules helps investor clients find success in meeting their stated goals. The strategy is designed to seek income from dividend-paying stocks and by opportunistically writing covered calls on those stocks. Although we maintain a 5% maximum allocation to our positions, here are examples of our October 2021 holdings: UnitedHealth Group Inc., Walmart Inc., Nike Inc., McDonald's Corp.,

Visa Inc., Caterpillar Inc., Home Depot Inc., Apple Inc., Microsoft Corp., and Goldman Sachs Group Inc., Procter & Gamble or Johnson & Johnson – all a result of this carefully implemented strategy.

Risk

To manage risk in investing, one must not only manage the downside of investments, but also make it the foundation for what they do. It's worth reiterating the Ben Graham philosophy when it comes to this element of investment strategy: Manage risk via the downside of a portfolio for the upside to take care of itself.

Returns

For the defined Three R's strategy to operate effectively, returns must be consistent with set expectations. When markets are up, participation in the upmarket is essential. But far more importantly, when markets are down or flat, managing the risks and mitigating the downside capture is crucial.

This, of course, is hinged on prudent choice of investments in high-quality companies that have great management and that pay dividends.

Separately Managed Account (SMA) strategies

The ability to adapt to change is crucial. CWP positions itself as an industry leader when implementing covered call strategies on our proprietary Enhanced Dividend Income Portfolio and concentrated equity holdings.

Tactical transition overlay

CWP specializes in the tactical transition of concentrated equity holdings. This process can be spread out over several years for tax-sensitive investors. Concentrated positions have calls written against the shares that the investor is willing to sell and recognize taxes on.

At Capital Wealth Planning, we provide time-tested conservative strategies using covered call writing designed to enhance income and overall total return.

Our flagship portfolio strategies

- Enhanced Dividend Income Portfolio (EDIP)
- Amplify's Enhanced Dividend Income ETF (Symbol: DIVO)

Our complementary portfolio strategies

- ESG Enhanced Dividend Income Portfolio
- Concentrated Stock Transition Overlay Strategy

Enhanced Dividend Income Portfolio

Geared toward people and organizations with at least $250,000 to invest, our Enhanced Dividend Income Portfolio is designed to offer a higher total return on a risk-adjusted basis for relatively conservative growth and income-oriented investors. We achieve this by constructing a portfolio that's diversified among all S&P sectors and by selling call options tactically to generate additional income.

Analyzing the sectors helps us determine what areas of the market are doing best by considering the strength relative to the overall market.

The Enhanced Dividend Income Portfolio has been designed for high-net-worth (HNW) and ultra-high-net-worth (UHNW) individuals and perpetual funds such as foundations and endowments that have income needs or spending policies in the range of 4-6% annualized. With the use of out-of-the-money staggered covered-call writing techniques, each position within the portfolio maintains a level of market exposure that allows additional capital appreciation in each of the underlying holdings.

> **Tactical difference**
>
> To increase your potential upside, CWP sells call options tactically versus keeping all positions covered.

CWP actively manages sector allocation and opportunities to participate in defensive and cyclical trends given the relevant economic cycle. We screen for high-quality growth and value stocks with strong fundamentals that have a history of increasing dividends.

The portfolio consists of blue-chip, dividend-paying stocks and is designed to deliver an estimated annual cash flow of 4-7% from dividend and option income, as well as the potential for capital appreciation.

Unlike a systematic covered-call program, CWP isn't obligated to continuously cover each individual equity position. When one of the underlying stocks demonstrates strength or an increase in implied volatility, our

BACKSTORY:

The confused mind usually says no.

Before founding Capital Wealth Planning, I worked at a firm that was bought out by a larger entity. Since I had a two-year non-compete, I had a lot of time on my hands to look at charts and think about my next career move.

When we created Capital Wealth Planning's strategy, we built it with ETFs as the underlying components. Then, we added the covered call overlay to the actual ETFs, which I thought was a novel way of bringing a diversified portfolio on a risk-adjusted basis to financial advisors.

In 2012, we had a client that called and loved the covered call strategy but couldn't use ETFs. This was a Catholic organization that needed individual stocks that aligned with their values. I was smart enough to take the phone call and run with it. I was fortunate to be in the right place at the right time. I never confuse that with brilliance.

We built the portfolio using the exact tactical approach you're learning to covered call writing on dividend-paying stocks instead of ETFs (which we also discussed for newer investors). It became such an easy thing for clients to understand.

Our previous strategy, that we still run to this day, has a very small asset base. It's a great strategy, but it's very hard to explain. The confused mind usually says no. If we can show you a strategy that's really easy to understand, that's how you should invest. You

should know what you're doing.

That's how we constructed Capital Wealth Planning's Enhanced Dividend Income Portfolio. It's comprised of 25-30 really well-known, high-quality, blue-chip stocks that pay dividends. We add our tactical covered call writing methodology around it. It's an approach with no black box. No quant. Everything is rules-based from start to finish ... we call our approach The Three R's.

Ultimately, every single client has the transparency and technology to see everything that we do.

CWP managers identify that opportunity and sell call options tactically, rather than keeping all positions covered and limiting potential upside across the board.

Covered calls on large-cap, dividend-growth, blue-chip U.S. companies

The CWP Enhanced Dividend Income Portfolio is suitable for qualified accounts, foundations, trusts, endowments, religious, and socially conscious investors. The portfolio offers strength and stability through a diversified portfolio of large-cap, high-quality, blue-chip companies that can stand the test of time. You receive regular dividend payments, which are suitable alternatives to fixed income products.

Writing covered calls provides a relatively conservative method to enhance cash flow and modestly reduce risk on the underlying equity portfolio. As interest rates increase, bond values go down, thus stimulating the need for an additional income source. Our focus on enhancing returns with dividends and option premiums won't change regardless of the market environment.

Stay the course

At CWP, our investment philosophy and processes remain the same, no matter what's happening in the market.

Our Enhanced Dividend Income Portfolio (EDIP) process

The process consists of four steps: identifying opportunities with dividend growers, diversifying with sector allocation, protecting the downside with security selection, and increasing total return with tactical covered call writing.

Step 1: Identifying opportunities with dividend growers

Seek and identify large-cap, high-quality, blue-chip companies primarily from the S&P 100 that can sustain their earnings and cash flow growth; and increase their dividend over time. Each candidate must have a liquid option chain. For example, our Enhanced Dividend Income Portfolio is managed with a strong emphasis on owning blue-chip DOW 30 and S&P 100 components with historical dividend and earnings growth. Why this focus? Because companies that grow dividends have historically done very well compared to the rest of the market with significantly less volatility.

Step 2: Diversifying with sector allocation

Construct a diversified portfolio that is concentrated by selecting approximately 25 - 30 holdings from our universe. Allocate across all sectors and look for individual stocks that are outperforming relative to their sector peers. We design our portfolio with the objective of achieving competitive returns when compared to broad market indices, while reducing volatility. This is accomplished by constructing an asset allocation that is relatively inclusive of all the traditional 10 S&P sectors to maintain diversification.

Step 3: Protecting the downside with security selection

Seek to lower risk and enhance total return by selling short-term call options tactically. In our portfolio design, we aren't obligated to cover each individual position 100 percent of the time – a real differentiator in the marketplace of covered call writing managers. We seek to provide 4 - 7% of gross income from dividend income and option premium, plus the potential for capital appreciation. We filter the universe by qualitative factors to find suitable candidates within each of the traditional S&P 500 sectors. Once we've reached roughly 40 to 60 candidates, we approach the list with both fundamental and technical analysis to determine which candidates offer attractive risk to return over a 6- to 12-month period.

Step 4: Increasing total return with tactical covered call writing

Here's where your portfolio works for you. By entering into contracts to sell our investments at a higher price, we earn consistent income and increase the total risk-adjustment return of the portfolio. Either use this income for living expenses or reinvest the proceeds back into the portfolio to increase returns. Our Enhanced Dividend Income Portfolio deploys a relatively conservative, tactical, covered call overlay that isn't obligated to continuously cover each individual equity position. When one of the underlying stocks demonstrate strength or an increase in implied volatility, our managers identify that opportunity and sell call options tactically, rather than keeping all positions covered and limiting potential upside. That's the key!

BACKSTORY:

In our worst nightmares, no one expected or planned for a pandemic to shut down the world.

Although we were all navigating the black swan event of COVID, the way the stock markets behaved during the 2020 correction was reminiscent of previous corrections. It was almost identical to the 2008 - 2009 pullback in the way it affected the options market and volatility.

Even though the event itself was unique, my investing rules remained the same, and experience shows that it's most important to follow these rules in times of extreme duress. From an investment perspective, I didn't have to scramble to know what to do. In fact, I knew what to do because

I had already done it. From a portfolio standpoint, the COVID correction wasn't treated any differently than other corrections. I knew what to do because I've done it before.

There will be another event that causes the stock market to crash and cascade, and most won't know what to do at that point. However, following the investing rules and principles you learned in this book will help you navigate those uncharted waters. You'll know what to do because you'll have done it before.

As mentioned previously, the Enhanced Dividend Income Portfolio (EDIP) has been designed for HNW and UHNW individuals and perpetual funds such as Foundations & Endowments that have income needs or spending policies in the range of 4-6% annualized. With the use of out-of-the-money staggered covered-call writing techniques, each position within the portfolio maintains a level of market exposure that allows additional capital appreciation in each of the underlying holdings. You can access us through your financial advisor, or you can look at the Amplify CWP ETF (symbol: DIVO).

On a final note

Being wealthy is much more than having money in the bank. It's also about having the freedom to make individual choices, to say yes or no, and to feel free to walk away from things that aren't a good fit for you. Being wealthy means you have money to take care of emergencies and known expenses such as your child's college education or helping pay for a house, in addition to cash flow for medical expenses, education, housing, retirement, and travel plans. With financial security, you have confidence knowing you're prepared for the storms of life and can enjoy the high moments. It means that you're ready for emergencies, while also earning money for your future.

What's more, being wealthy empowers you to take care of your loved ones, from your spouse, children, family, and friends to your community, colleagues, and the world at large.

When you're rich, you're also free to enjoy conscious spending and pursue your individual goals, whatever they may be.

As you become great at managing your finances and growing your wealth, you can pass along your knowledge to your loved ones and help lift them up and improve their lives. You can have a tremendous effect on others through your own successful financial management and by continuing to help those around you.

I sincerely hope that you feel inspired and educated to take the next step on your financial journey to living the life you deserve.

IMPORTANT INFORMATION

Methodologies of the Morningstar rating for SMAs

We've been building and managing proprietary income-oriented portfolios since 2005. Our Enhanced Dividend Income SMA strategy accounts for roughly $200 million of CWP's more than $4 billion under management.

Morningstar's rating for separate accounts offers a clear, quantitative assessment based on past performance that includes both return and risk, measured via a rating of one to five stars. This helps investors determine the risk-adjusted returns for separate account composites.

Investor benefits

• **Easy to identify:** It gives investors the ability to quickly identify and compare separate accounts to research.

• **Familiar rating approach:** Morningstar's rating for separate accounts builds on its existing 5-star tool already in use by many investors for open-end mutual fund, closed-end fund, and variety annuity research.

• **Identify valuable management teams:** Using this rating also helps identify management teams that are adding value over time. This rating is intended for use as the initial step in investment evaluation.

It's important to note that the rating is an objective grade of demonstrated performance and not designed to anticipate future performance.

Five stars

Capital Wealth Planning received a 5-Star Morningstar™ rating for its Enhanced Dividend Income SMA among 28 peer option writing SMAs in the category for 2017-2021.

Expected utility approach

The Morningstar rating also uses an enhanced risk-adjusted return measure based on "expected utility theory," which accounts for all variations in a separate account's monthly performance, with more emphasis on downward variation.

Star ratings

This methodology ranks separate accounts by their Morningstar risk-adjusted return scores. Morningstar assigns stars using this scale:

* 10%

** 22.5%

*** 35%

**** 22.5%
***** 10%

Separate accounts are ranked against others in the same Morningstar category.
Categories are assigned based on extensive holdings-based portfolio analysis.
There are three time periods for ratings — three, five, and 10 years for separate
accounts. These ratings are weighted and combined to produce the overall Morningstar rating. Morningstar will not calculate ratings for categories or time periods
that contain fewer than five separate accounts.

Since separate accounts don't have sales loads or multiple share classes, corresponding adjustments for the mutual fund rating are not applicable to the separate account rating. There are differences between the separate account rating
methodology and the rating methodologies for other investments because of the
unique way that separate account managers calculate and report investment performance.

All separate account performance data is reported to Morningstar as a "composite" of similarly managed portfolios. Morningstar rates separate accounts
based on total returns that haven't been adjusted for investment management
fees. Morningstar does not tax-adjust the returns of separate accounts that invest
in municipal bonds.

Composites

Finally, investors who have the same separate account may have different portfolio holdings because each investor has individually customized account needs,
security preferences, and tax considerations. Separate account managers calculate and report composite returns for each investment style they offer. Since the
method for calculating composites can vary, Morningstar will calculate ratings for
only those firms that report composites according to the guidelines of the Association for Investment Management and Research (AIMR). This helps ensure that
ratings are fairly assigned and transparent. Roughly 90% of the separate accounts
in Morningstar's database come from AIMR-compliant firms.

Returns for DJIA and CWP EDIP are adjusted for dividends and splits and
are calculated on a total-return basis gross of management fees. Raw data was
provided by djaverages.com and Bloomberg. Inception date for EDIP WRAP is
1/1/2013. Past performance doesn't guarantee future results. The model portfolio contains equity stocks that are managed with a view toward capital appreciation and income. An investor can't invest directly in an index. CWP's EDIP and
the DJIA have similar volatility and the index acts as an appropriate benchmark
for this strategy.

Historically, reinvestment of dividends and option income generally are not guaranteed and a company's future ability to pay dividends may be limited.

EDIP disclosures

Capital Wealth Planning, LLC claims compliance with the Global Investment Performance Standards (GIPS®) and has prepared and presented this report in compliance with the GIPS standards. Capital Wealth Planning, LLC has been independently verified for the periods Jan 2010 thru Sept 2017. The verification report(s) is/are available upon request. Verification assesses whether (1) the firm has complied with all the composite construction requirements of the GIPS standards on a firm-wide basis and (2) the firm's policies and procedures are designed to calculate and present performance in compliance with the GIPS standards. Verification does not ensure the accuracy of any specific composite presentation. The verification and performance examination reports are available upon request.

ACKNOWLEDGEMENTS

I have to start by thanking my family: JoAnna, Jack, and Dallas, who I'm so thankful to share my life with. My grandparents, Babcia and Pop Pop, mom and dad, and Granni and Poppy (my in-laws) ... the generations before me who shared their wisdom and values. Bill Bierlin, my early mentor, who treated me like family.

Throughout my career, there have been many memorable names, including Dave Hirsch and Kevin Jajuga who worked with me in the early days at W.H. Newbolds. We trained together and got our licenses on the same day. There are enough stories from those first few years that could make another book. Floyd Carl, who I worked with at Newbolds and Wheat First — if I only knew then what I know now.

At Capital Wealth Planning, I have to give a nod to Josh Smith, George Raffa, Jack Fisher, Jeff Saut, Carlos Figueroa, Kesia Sondrini, Jodi Phillips, Samantha Thomas, Yerania Barrios, Ryan Carney, Ryland Mathews, Lou Albenga, Keith Wagner, Kent Elwell, Ken Coffman, and Josh Miller.

Industry legends: Gary Kaminsky for his kindness and insights, and Susan Krakower for her relentless commitment to our vision. Anthony Scaramucci and Jackie DeAngelis for believing in the methodology and spreading the word.

My creative and marketing leadership team: Jackie Walling, Ryan Dawson, Lindsay White, and Jay Coulter, who brought my vision to life.

I'd like to thank Amber Vilhauer and her team at NGNG for their tremendous work and for keeping everything on schedule.

Kevin Simpson is Founder and Chief Investment Officer of Capital Wealth Planning (CWP). Based in Naples, Florida, CWP is an SEC-registered fee-only investment advisory firm. The company has more than $4 billion of assets under management, and has been building and managing equity income-oriented portfolios since 2005.

Originally from Philadelphia, Kevin has been investing in options since beginning his career at W.H. Newbold's Sons & Co. in 1992. He worked for seven years at Wheat First Butcher Singer (later Wells Fargo) where he helped institutions and high-net-worth individuals plan and achieve their financial goals through option-centered strategies. He also worked at Sterling Financial for several years before opening CWP.

Kevin practices the strategies outlined in this book, applying institutional investment management to diversified equity and option portfolios. His methodologies are designed to enhance risk-adjusted returns and offer portfolio protection while delivering monthly cash flow.

CWP leads the implementation of covered call strategies with their Enhanced Dividend Income Portfolio, ESG Enhanced Dividend Income Portfolio, ETF Covered Call Portfolio, and Covered Call Overlay Service, and was recognized by Financial Advisor Magazine in 2018, 2019 and 2021 as one of the top 50 fastest-growing SEC-registered investment advisors in the country. To learn more, visit www.capitalwealthplanning.com.

A frequent contributor on Yahoo Finance, Fox Business, and CNBC, Kevin also hosts a podcast where he interviews the financial industry's top investment professionals to provide expert insight and analysis for a deeper understanding of today's markets.

He graduated from George Washington University, where he majored in finance. Kevin lives in Naples, Florida, with his wife JoAnna. They have one son, Jack, and Dallas the dog.